T0303958

Global Marketing
Co-Operation and Networks

Global Marketing Co-Operation and Networks has been co-published simultaneously as *Journal of Euromarketing*, Volume 9, Number 2 2000.

The *Journal of Euromarketing* Monographic "Separates"

Below is a list of "separates," which in serials librarianship means a special issue simultaneously published as a special journal issue or double-issue *and* as a "separate" hardbound monograph. (This is a format which we also call a "DocuSerial.")

"Separates" are published because specialized libraries or professionals may wish to purchase a specific thematic issue by itself in a format which can be separately cataloged and shelved, as opposed to purchasing the journal on an on-going basis. Faculty members may also more easily consider a "separate" for classroom adoption.

"Separates" are carefully classified separately with the major book jobbers so that the journal tie-in can be noted on new book order slips to avoid duplicate purchasing.

You may wish to visit Haworth's website at . . .

http://www.HaworthPress.com

. . . to search our online catalog for complete tables of contents of these separates and related publications.

You may also call 1-800-HAWORTH (outside US/Canada: 607-722-5857), or Fax: 1-800-895-0582 (outside US/Canada: 607-771-0012), or e-mail at:

getinfo@haworthpressinc.com

Global Marketing Co-Operation and Networks, edited by Leo Paul Dana, BA, MBA, PhD (Vol. 9, No. 2, 2000). *"EXCELLENT . . . . WELL-REFERENCED . . . . VERY USEFUL. I for one have found it to be current, effective, and useful for developing my own research and teaching materials." (Claudio Vignali, BA, MPhil, DipM, Senior Lecturer, Manchester Metropolitan University, United Kingdom)*

Cross-National Consumer Psychographics, edited by Lynn R. Kahle (Vol. 8, No. 1/2, 1999). *"Cross-National Consumer Psychographics provides marketing professionals and students with data from several applications around the world of the list of values (LOV), so you can consider the implications for understanding consumers cross-culturally. Through this unique book you will find how different countries and different individual consumers may be segmented based on their social values so you can develop the best marketing strategies for your products."*

Newer Insights into Marketing: Cross-Cultural and Cross-National Perspectives, edited by Camille P. Schuster, PhD, and Phil Harris, BA (Hons) (Vol. 7, No. 2, 1999). *This new book analyzes and investigates international marketing strategies to determine effective marketing practices of businesses in the global arena.*

Green Marketing in a Unified Europe, edited by Alma T. Mintu-Wimsatt, PhD, and Héctor R. Lozada, PhD (Vol. 5, No. 3, 1996). *"Takes a well-researched and heartfelt approach to the 3 P's of environmental marketing–preservation, protection, and proactive product development." (Debbie Thorne, PhD, Director, Center for Ethics, The University of Tampa)*

International Joint Ventures in East Asia, edited by Roger Baran, PhD, Yigang Pan, PhD, and Erdener Kaynak, PhD, DSc (Vol. 4, No. 3/4, 1996). *"A valuable resource for anyone interested in joint ventures anywhere in the world." (Sunder Narayanan, PhD, Assistant Professor, School of Business, Columbia University)*

Ethical Issues in International Marketing, edited by Nejdet Delener, PhD (Vol. 4, No. 2, 1995). *"Provides an invaluable education to the reader and encourages the reader to think about important issues that increasingly confront businesspeople in their dealings within a global marketplace." (George V. Priovolos, PhD, CPA, Assistant Professor, Marketing Department, Hagan School of Business, Iona College)*

The Impact of Innovation and Technology in the Global Marketplace, edited by Shaker A. Zahra, PhD, and Abbas J. Ali, PhD (Vol. 3, No. 3/4, 1994). *"The editors have captured the excitement of the present day technological innovations with a wise selection of scholarly articles. Grab this book and read it before it's too late!" (Raymond A. K. Cox, PhD, Professor of Finance, Central Michigan University)*

Global Marketing Co-Operation and Networks

Leo Paul Dana, BA, MBA, PhD
Editor

Global Marketing Co-Operation and Networks has been co-published simultaneously as *Journal of Euromarketing*, Volume 9, Number 2 2000.

Routledge
Taylor & Francis Group

NEW YORK AND LONDON

First Published by

International Business Press®, 10 Alice Street, Binghamton, NY 13904-1580 USA

This edition published 2011 by Routledge
711 Third Avenue, New York, NY 10017
2 Park Square, Milton Park, Abingdon, Oxon, OX14 4RN

Global Marketing Co-Operation and Networks has been co-published simultaneously as *Journal of Euromarketing* ™, Volume 9, Number 2 2000.

Cover design by Thomas J. Mayshock Jr.

Library of Congress Cataloging-in-Publication Data

Global marketing co-operation and networks / Leo Paul Dana, editor.
      p. cm.
      "Co-published simultaneously as Journal of Euromarketing, volume 9, number 2, 2000."
      Includes bibliographical references and index.
      ISBN 0-7890-1302-9 (alk. paper)–ISBN 0-7890-1303-7 (alk. paper)
      1. Internet marketing. 2. Export marketing. I. Dana, Leo Paul.
HF5415.1265 .G58 2000
658.8'48–dc21
                                             00-063372

Publisher's Note
The publisher has gone to great lengths to ensure the quality of this reprint but points out that some imperfections in the original may be apparent.

Global Marketing Co-Operation and Networks

CONTENTS

ABOUT THE EDITOR

Leo Paul Dana, a graduate of McGill University and of the Ecole des Hautes Etudes Commerciales, was, until 1999, Deputy Director of the International Business MBA Programme at Nanyang Business School in Singapore. He has since joined the University of Canterbury, in New Zealand.

He began lecturing at Concordia University in 1984, and in 1985 he was appointed Expert Witness to the Government of Canada, House of Commons Standing Committee on Transport. From 1992 to 1997 he designed and taught graduate courses at McGill University where he also produced fifteen documentaries about culture and enterprise. In 1997, he pioneered, with Professor Richard Wright, McGill's first summer session in Asia, taking undergraduate and MBA students to Hong Kong and Vietnam. Later, a second group of McGill students went to Asia, and took a course with Professor Dana in Singapore.

Among Professor Dana's other short-term projects, he has done consulting for the Economic Committee of the Senate of Romania, and has served several times as Visiting Professor at the Graduate School of Management, in Nancy, France. More recently, he was Visiting Professor for the University of Pittsburgh. As well, he taught International Business in Romania, where he served as Visiting Professor in the Canadian MBA Programme at the Academie des Sciences Economiques in Bucharest. He has also been Visiting Professor at INSEAD.

He has been keynote speaker in Addis Ababa, Athens, Bangkok, Beijing, Cairo, Delhi, and Montreal. About 100 of his scholastic works appear in leading refereed journals, including *Entrepreneurship: Theory & Practice,* and the *Journal of Small Business Management.* He serves as regional editor for the *Journal of International Business & Entrepreneurship*, and he is on the editorial executive board of *Entrepreneurship, Innovation, and Change*, as well as on the advisory board of *The Journal of Enterprising Culture.* He has served as Guest Editor for the *British Food Journal, International Journal of Entrepreneurship & Innovation Management, International Journal of Technology Management, Management Case Quarterly*, and *Small Business Economics.*

As indicated in the *Canadian Who's Who*, Dr. Dana is Senior Advisor to the World Association for Small & Medium Enterprises. His books include: *Entrepreneurship and the Service Industries*; *Enterprising in the Global Environment* (3 editions); *Perspectives of Enterprise*; *Tourism: Business and Practice*; *Tradewinds: Cross-Cultural Issues in International Marketing*; and *Entrepreneurship in Pacific Asia: Past, Present & Future*. His webpage site is: http://professordana.homestead. com/1.html.

Preface

In 1997, I was approached to become involved in an emerging field of research, international entrepreneurship. Richard Wright and Hamid Etemad were organising the first conference of its kind, by invitation only. Thus, I came to be the Keynote Speaker at the First International Conference on Globalization and Emerging Businesses, which took place at McGill University, September 25-28, 1998. Out of this came the book *International Entrepreneurship: Globalization of Emerging Businesses*, edited by Professor Richard W. Wright, and published by JAI Press in 1999.

The success of the first conference led to interest in a follow-up. More and more universities were introducing courses about international entrepreneurship and about globalisation. I therefore took it upon myself to organise a second world conference on the theme of Internationalisation of Entrepreneurship. This took place at the Goodwood Park Hotel, in Singapore, August 15-18, 1999. Since the international- isation of entrepreneurs usually takes place through co-operation and networking, our focus was Global Marketing Co-operation and Networks.

The turnout was beyond our expectations, and many participants asked about buying reprints of papers for use as course materials. More and more academics began showing a growing interest in Global Marketing and Networks. Professor Erdener Kaynak wisely recognised this, and commissioned me to assemble this special volume suitable for university course use.

The first article is a conceptual think-piece, including a literature

Leo Paul Dana is Senior Advisor, World Association for Small & Medium Enterprises, and affiliated with the University of Canterbury in New Zealand.

[Haworth co-indexing entry note]: "Preface." Dana, Leo Paul. Co-published simultaneously in *Journal of Euromarketing* (International Business Press, an imprint of The Haworth Press, Inc.) Vol. 9, No. 2, 2000, pp. xvii-xviii; and: *Global Marketing Co-Operation and Networks* (ed: Leo Paul Dana) International Business Press, an imprint of The Haworth Press, Inc., 2000, pp. xi-xii. Single or multiple copies of this article are available for a fee from The Haworth Document Delivery Service [1-800-342-9678, 9:00 a.m. - 5:00 p.m. (EST). E-mail address: getinfo@haworthpressinc.com].

review. The subsequent collection of articles includes empirical research as well as conceptual material. Authors include leading researchers from the United States, Canada, England, Norway, Australia and New Zealand.

The collection provides a framework for grasping important research findings about global marketing co-operation and networks, and about the impact of these on the inevitable internationalisation of entrepreneurs.

I would like to express my appreciation to Dr. Erdener Kaynak for providing the opportunity to disseminate a significant attempt at integration of knowledge about global marketing co-operation and networks. The articles will doubtless be useful in stimulating future research.

Leo Paul Dana

The Global Reach of Symbiotic Networks

Leo Paul Dana
Hamid Etemad
Richard W. Wright

SUMMARY. The nature of marketing is changing. Competition in international markets was traditionally the realm of large companies, with smaller businesses remaining local or regional in scope. In today's global economy, increased specialisation has led multinationals to outsource to small firms. Thus, large firms are forming alliances with networks of small businesses. Hence, by allowing multinationals to perform marketing functions for them, small firms are internationalising more than ever before. Such recent developments provide new internationalisation opportunities for smaller firms. *[Article copies available for a fee from The Haworth Document Delivery Service: 1-800-342-9678. E-mail address: <getinfo@haworthpressinc.com> Website: <http://www.HaworthPress.com>]*

KEYWORDS. Internationalisation, out-sourcing, alliances, marketing, niche, networks

INTRODUCTION

International marketing, today, involves networks and alliances in which small firms are playing an important role. Reynolds (1997)

Leo Paul Dana is affiliated with the University of Canterbury, New Zealand. Hamid Etemad is affiliated with McGill University. Richard W. Wright is The E. Claiborne Robins Distinguished University Chair at the University of Richmond.

[Haworth co-indexing entry note]: "The Global Reach of Symbiotic Networks." Dana, Leo Paul, Hamid Etemad, and Richard W. Wright. Co-published simultaneously in *Journal of Euromarketing* (International Business Press, an imprint of The Haworth Press, Inc.) Vol. 9, No. 2, 2000, pp. 1-16; and: *Global Marketing Co-Operation and Networks* (ed: Leo Paul Dana) International Business Press, an imprint of The Haworth Press, Inc., 2000, pp. 1-16. Single or multiple copies of this article are available for a fee from The Haworth Document Delivery Service [1-800-342-9678, 9:00 a.m. - 5:00 p.m. (EST). E-mail address: getinfo@haworthpressinc.com].

1

noted that the recent expansion of markets has not been associated with an expansion of the role of larger firms. Instead, smaller firms are filling niche roles (Buckley, 1997). Consequently, international marketing has evolved to include networks comprised of both large and small firms.

As discussed by Harrison (1997), the development of networks is a significant trend, as the product of a small firm can now be easily distributed globally. Bonaccorsi (1992) and Dana and Etemad (1994; 1995) explained how small businesses can delegate internationalisation activities to larger firms. Such developments are fusing elements of international business with small business/entrepreneurship.

As an older discipline, international business has developed a cumulative methodological and theoretical tradition of its own. Several theories deserve special attention. Among these, Vernon's (1966; 1979) Product Life Cycle (PLC) theory attempts to explain world trade and foreign direct investment (FDI) in manufactured products, on the basis of stages in a product's life. Historically, the PLC theory was quite powerful in explaining patterns of international trade and investment in many manufacturing sectors. It does, however, have limits. Viewed from an Asian or European perspective, Vernon's argument that most new products are developed and produced in the United States seems ethnocentric. While it may have been true during the period of American dominance, it is less true today when product innovations are occurring elsewhere as well, and when a number of new products are now introduced simultaneously in the United States, Japan, and Europe.

Moreover, some products may, because of very rapid innovation, have extremely short life cycles, rendering it impossible to achieve cost reductions by moving production from one country to another. While the theory applies well to some products, it has little relevance to vertically integrated industries dominated by intra-industry trade, or to countries where the local market is too small to sustain economies of scale, forcing firms to internationalise from their beginnings, in order to survive.

Modern monopolistic advantage/market imperfection theory arises from Hymer's 1960 thesis (1976). He demonstrated that FDI occurred largely in oligopolistic industries rather than in industries operating in near-perfect competition. Caves (1971) expanded on this to show that superior knowledge permitted the investing firm to produce differentiated products that consumers would prefer to similar, locally-made goods and this would give the firm some control over the selling price and an advantage over indigenous firms. To support these contentions, he noted that companies investing overseas were in industries that typically engaged in heavy product research and marketing efforts. The internalisation theory expounded by Buckley and Casson (1976), and others, is an extension of the market imperfection theory. The multinational is assumed to hold a monopoly control over technological, marketing or management know-how. A shortcoming with the internalisation theory lies in its choice of industry-specific factors as the primary emphasis with respect to the internationalisation decision. The theory does not necessarily explain decisions of entrepreneurs to set up enterprises in locations as a function of personal preference for a particular environment–certain locations may be preferred by an entrepreneur for religious, linguistic, cultural or personal reasons. To the entrepreneur, these are all constituent (albeit non-monetary) costs not captured by economic-based theories such as internalisation. Dunning's (1973; 1977; 1980; 1988) eclectic paradigm provided a framework designed to extend the internalisation theories to explain how location factors influence the nature and direction of FDI. Agarwal and Ramaswami (1992) used firm size as a measure to operationalise this paradigm.

Knickerbocker (1973) postulated that in oligopolistic industries, enterprises "react" to each other's moves, and imitate each other such as to reduce the risk of being different. This came to be known as the oligopolistic reaction theory. Two findings formed the basis of his theory: the first referred to evidence indicating the tendency of firms in a number of American industries to cluster together their direct investments in foreign countries; the second originated from data indicating that American enterprises in the forefront of international expansion are typically in industries dominated by oligopolies. A problem with this theory, however, is that it does not apply to international entrepreneurs. As explained by Schumpeter (1911), entrepreneurs create and innovate: they often have first-mover instincts for taking advantage of present opportunities. Such behaviour is not explained adequately by the oligopolistic reaction theory.

The Uppsala Model (Johanson and Wiedersheim-Paul, 1975) identified four stages of entry into international markets. This was elaborated in Johanson and Vahlne (1977). Bilkey and Tesar (1977) opted for a six-stage model. Newbould, Buckley and Thurwell (1978) also examined such a stage approach to international business. Cavusgil (1980; 1984) considered five stages. Bartlett and Ghoshal (1989) were among others to adhere to this school of thought. A major problem of this approach is that it assumes a span of time through which the various stages evolve in a controlled fashion. Yet, international new ventures, as one example, represent entrepreneurial behaviour that cannot possibly follow these incremental stages. Often, a firm in a vertically integrated industry must internationalise immediately, because its domestic market is too small to sustain it. In such cases, there are no time-delayed increments to the process. The same is true of many small businesses with a high-tech product or demand conditions defying conventional patterns. Coviello and Munro (1993) found that small, high-tech firms rarely follow the stepwise approach to internationalisation.

THE GLOBALISATION OF ENTREPRENEURSHIP

Governments around the world have accepted that entrepreneurship contributes to development, with a positive effect on society, creating employment, economic expansion, a larger tax base, and more consumer well-being. This has led to a rich literature about entrepreneurship in Africa (Brockhaus, 1991; Dana, 1993); Asia (Chen, 1997; Dana, 1987; 1999; Fan, Chen and Kirby, 1996; Gadgil, 1959; Geertz, 1963; Hazlehurst, 1966; Morita and Oliga, 1991; Ojuka-Onedo, 1996; Patel, 1987; Sarder, Ghosh, and Rosa, 1997; Tambunan, 1992; Wimalatissa, 1996), Europe (Boissevain and Grotenbreg, 1987; Dana, 1992; 1998; Gibb, 1986-7; Hisrich and Fulop, 1995; Hisrich and Vecsenyi, 1990; Holmquist and Sundin, 1988; Liuhto, 1996; Martin and Grbac, 1998; Noar, 1985; Pache, 1996; Walsh and Anderson, 1995); North America (Dana, 1990; 1995; Grabinsky, 1996; Silva-Castan, Prott and Anjola-Rojas, 1997), and South America (Dana, 1994; 1997; Raghunanda, 1995).

In any country, it used to be that an entrepreneur who wished to avoid uncertainties inherent in foreign markets could simply keep a business local by refraining from expanding internationally, thereby avoiding the risks of facing foreign competition. However, opportunities for entrepreneurship are becoming less restricted to domestic markets. Protective tariffs are being reduced and business travel is becoming easier. Technology is also facilitating trade. Thus, international business is rapidly becoming a concern for entrepreneurship and so, too, entrepreneurship for international business. As explained by Oviatt and McDougall, "facile use of low-cost communication technology and transportation means that the ability to discover and take advantage of business opportunities in multiple countries is not the preserve of large, mature corporations" (1994, p. 46). These trends, coupled with decreasing government protection in many countries, are enabling new entrants to join the competitive field and are causing multinationals to seek ever-greater efficiency.

Large, established firms are increasingly finding this efficiency by subcontracting to smaller businesses, owned and managed by entrepreneurs. There is a new symbiosis between large and small business, with the large firms providing new niche opportunities for the smaller firms. Such relationships have long characterised economies such as Japan (Wright, 1989) and Korea (Dana, 1999), and are increasingly apparent in North America and Europe. The accelerating trend toward internationalisation presents unprecedented opportunities, challenges and threats for entrepreneurs and their firms.

MARKETING AND NETWORKS

In the area of international marketing, the export behaviour of small firms has been studied extensively (Anderson, 1995; Bilkey, 1978; Brush, 1995; Cavusgil, Bilkey and Tesar, 1979; Dichtl, Leibold, Köglmayer and Müller, 1984; Tesar and Tarleton, 1982). Aaby and Slater (1989) reviewed 55 export studies. Dichtl, Leibold, Koeglmayr and Mueller (1990) conducted an extensive study comparing German, Finnish, Japanese, South African and South Korean firms; they concluded that an important determinant of export performance was the foreign market orientation of decision-makers. Simon (1992) found successful entrepreneurs in Germany to have a customer orientation. Adams and Hall (1993) studied 1,132 small and medium enterprises across Europe; personal factors were found to be important causal variables of export performance. Cavusgil and Kirpalani (1993) linked export success to a favourable management attitude and commitment to export. Other studies examined licensing and foreign direct investment by entrepreneurs. Carstairs and Welch (1982) suggested that the key success factor for licensing among entrepreneurs was the development of effective interaction with the licensee, in a long-term relationship. This led to market information as well as commercial viability. Contractor (1990) found that among 241 American companies, licensing was a profitable alternative to foreign direct investment; this was increased by the desire for rapid market penetration amidst constraints arising from trade policy and international risk. Sherman (1996) addressed international franchising, and suggested strategies for international co-operation.

Meanwhile, sociologists developed a very rich literature about entrepreneurship networks. Networking involves calling upon a web of contacts for information, support and assistance. Aldrich and Zimmer (1986) integrated social network theory into the study of entrepreneurship; they linked entrepreneurship to social networks. Carsrud, Gaglio and Olm (1986) also found networks important to the understanding of new venture development. Boissevain and Grotenbreg (1987), in their study of the Surinamese in Amsterdam, suggested that access to a network of contacts is an important resource for entrepreneurs; this study noted, among other things, that networks can provide introductions to wholesalers and warnings of government inspections. Aldrich, Rosen and Woodward (1987) found network accessibility to be significant in predicting new venture creation. Dubini and Aldrich (1991) found networks central to entrepreneurship. In their study of Koreans in Atlanta, Min and Jaret (1985) found family networks to be a source of manpower for entrepreneurs. Analysing Asian entrepreneurs in Britain, Aldrich, Jones and McEvoy found that Asian entrepreneurs "benefit from . . . certain advantages denied non-ethnic competitors" (1984, p. 193). Auster and Aldrich (1984) concluded that the ethnic enclave reduces the vulnerability of small firms, by providing an ethnic market and also general social and economic support, including credit. Related research was done by Cummings (1980), Light (1972; 1984), Light and Bonacich (1988), Ward (1987), Ward and Jenkins (1984), Wong (1987) and Wu (1983).

Golden and Dollinger (1993), Larson (1991) and Lipparini and Sobrero (1994) found that high growth firms were involved in networks. Anderson (1995) and Johanson and Associates (1994) examined the effect of business networks on internationalisation of firms. It appears that networks can positively affect a firm's degree of internationalisation. Golden and Dollinger (1993) linked success to co-operative alliances; Larson (1991) did so to partner networks.

McGee and Dowling (1994) researched what they called co-operative arrangements. Shepherd (1991) used the term constellation; Tallman and Shenkar (1994) wrote of co-operative ventures. Welch (1992) addressed various types of alliances that assist small firms.

SYMBIOTIC MARKETING
BETWEEN LARGE AND SMALL FIRMS

In several industries, large and small firms are working together in networks, which facilitate international marketing. In the airline sector, for instance, it has become common for major international airlines to sub-contract and even to franchise to small firms. Also known as out-sourcing, sub-contracting involves an agreement in which one company contracts a specific segment of its business operations to another firm. This allows firms to focus on their competitive advantage, core competencies, and/or that which they choose to specialise. In the airline industry, larger international carriers equipped with fleets suitable for longer haul flights have been sub-contracting short-haul routes to small-scale carriers with turbo-prop aircraft. Significant cost reductions are achieved in terms of more specialised aircraft. Also, a small carrier may have the cost advantage of not being unionised.

Each scheduled airline has a two-letter airline identification code, which designates its flights. Allegheny Airlines pioneered the concept of sub-contracting flights to independent firms, to which it assigned its own two-letter designator. The airline developed a hub in Pittsburgh and introduced new routes. Deregulation allowed Allegheny Airlines to concentrate on its most profitable routes, using jet aircraft; yet, many other routes were still important as they provided feeder traffic and thus enlarged the customer base. Rather than discontinue service to minor airports, Allegheny maintained a network of small, independent carriers that would provide flights, under the brand name Allegheny Commuter, on behalf of Allegheny Airlines, under contract. Independent contractors included Chatauqua Airlines, Fischer Brothers Aviation, Henson, Ransome Airlines, South Jersey Airlines and Suburban Airlines. This enabled Allegheny Airlines (later USAir and more recently, USAirways) to focus on expanding its presence, without abandoning low-density routes to smaller communities. This concept proved beneficial to Allegheny, to its associated entrepreneurs such as Mr. and Mrs. Ransome, and to the public. The members of the

Allegheny network saved costs, which were subsequently reflected in their competitiveness, in terms of expanded network reach, lower ticket prices and higher satisfaction among customers who benefitted from versatile turbo-props. When Allegheny changed its name to US-Air, it kept the Allegheny Commuter network, which eventually became USAir Express. The benefits associated with this networking would soon impact the dynamics of airline competition, tempting others to emulate.

Trans World Airlines (formerly Transcontinental & Western Air, Inc.), also known as TWA, established the Trans World Express network of commuter feeders. Air Midwest, Resort Air and Resort Commuter provided this service. In addition, until being absorbed by US-Air, Piedmont Airlines had a code-sharing arrangement with TWA.

American Airlines originally opposed code-sharing, but launched its American Eagle program in November 1984. Members have included AVAir, Air Midwest, Chaparral Airlines, Command Airways, Executive Air Charter, Metro Express II, Metroflight, Simmons Airlines and Wings West Airlines.

Delta Air Lines, Inc. set up the Delta Connection, operated in 1985 by Atlantic Southeast Airlines, Comair, Ransome Airlines (formerly an independent contractor for the Allegheny Commuter network) and Rio Airways. Meanwhile, Skywest Airlines and South Central Air operated Western Express for Western Airlines. Both networks were combined when Delta absorbed Western, on April 1, 1987. Delta also set up a network operated by Business Express, using Delta's (DL) designator.

United Airlines Inc. started sharing its (UN) designator in 1985, with Appleton-based Air Wisconsin, Seattle-based Horizon Air and Fresno-based WestAir. In 1986, Aspen Airways (operating Convair 580 turbo-props between Denver and Aspen) became a United Airlines code-sharer too. United lost Horizon when this contractor was acquired by Alaska Airlines.

Deregulation spread to Canada and Europe, and so did the principle of creating alliances and networks among large, international airlines and small, local sub-contractors. In Canada, Air Canada set up a family of Air Canada Connectors, including Air Alliance, Air BC, Air Nova and Air Ontario, as well as Austin Airways (Canada's oldest airline, established as a family business in 1934). Eventually, several other small firms, including Alberta Citylink, British Midland, and

Central Mountain Air, also became code-share partners. Sub-contracting has proven to be an effective means of providing a specialised niche service in the airline industry.

Even the largest airlines in the world have felt the pressure to co-operate with network partners. The One World Alliance of American Airlines, British Airways, Canadian Airlines International, Cathay Pacific and Qantas, should be viewed as an oligopolistic reaction (Knickerbocker, 1973), to the Star Alliance. The noteworthy point is that all the small suppliers and commuter carriers attached to trunk airlines are participating in international markets.

International franchising is a more recent innovation in the quest to market airline services internationally. As is the case with sub-contracting, franchising is also an effective way by which an airline can expand beyond its own resource base. Like sub-contracting, a franchise agreement may allow, and usually does allow, the franchisee to use the franchiser's airline code and to operate aeroplanes painted in the livery of the franchiser. Unlike sub-contracting, franchising may allow an airline to enter the restrictive domestic markets of foreign countries, by using local franchisees.

In May 1996, British Airways Public Ltd. Co. signed its first franchise agreement with a small, regional carrier outside the United Kingdom. This allowed Sun-Air, a Danish airline, to paint its fleet in the livery of British Airways, and its cabin crew to wear British Airways uniforms. In July 1996, British Airways signed a franchise agreement with Comair, a small firm in the Republic of South Africa. In the case of airline franchising, the franchiser benefits from rapid expansion without heavy capital investment. It also bypasses barriers against foreign ownership. The franchisee benefits from the marketing distribution channels of the franchiser. For the entrepreneur who operates a small airline, franchising facilitates international marketing. Chen and Hambrick (1995) found that small airlines were more active than larger ones in initiating competitive moves, while large airlines acted in unexciting ways.

TOWARD THE FUTURE

Globalisation has begun to dismantle the barriers that traditionally separated local firms from multinationals. Local markets are becoming integral parts of broader markets. As market opportunities expand, the modus operandi of both small enterprises and larger firms is changing. Smaller enterprises can now take advantage of expanded markets. This is forcing multinational subsidiaries and their parent companies to adopt new strategic postures. Increased specialisation is allowing smaller firms to be niche players. Market-driven co-operation is such that multinationals out-source to smaller niche players. At the same time, small firms are using multinationals to perform the global marketing function. Consequently, as smaller firms are expanding and competing globally, multinationals are becoming more locally responsive. Their strategies are therefore converging.

Recent years have witnessed the evolution of a variety of joint-marketing strategies. In the airline industry, for instance, sub-contracting to a small firm allows a major airline to maintain an all-jet fleet, while out-sourcing short-haul routes. Franchising enables a franchiser to penetrate a protected market by using a local franchisee. Simultaneously, it provides a tiny franchisee with the opportunity to market internationally, via the franchiser's global network. The success of such alliances suggests that such co-operative marketing strategies may spread to other service industries.

REFERENCES

Aaby, Nils-Erik and Stanley F. Slater (1989), "Management Influence on Export Performance: A Review of Empirical Literature 1978-1988," *International Marketing Review* 6(4), pp. 7-26.

Adams, G. and G. Hall (1993), "Influences on the Growth of SMEs: An International Comparison," *Entrepreneurship and Regional Development* 5, pp. 73-84.

Agarwal, S. and S. Ramaswami (1992), "Choice of Foreign Market Entry Mode," *Journal of International Business Studies* 23(1), pp. 1-27.

Aldrich, Howard E., Trevor P. Jones, and David McEvoy (1984), "Ethnic Advantage and Minority Business Development," in Robin Ward and Richard Jenkins, eds., *Ethnic Communities in Business: Strategies for Economic Survival*, Cambridge: Cambridge University Press, pp. 189-210.

Aldrich, Howard, Ben Rosen and William Woodward (1987), "The Impact of Social Networks on Business Foundings and Profit in a Longitudinal Study," *Frontiers of Entrepreneurship Research*, Wellesley, Massachusetts: Babson College, pp. 154-168.

Aldrich, Howard E. and Catherine Zimmer (1986), "Entrepreneurship Through Social Networks," in Donald L. Sexton and Raymond W. Smilor, eds., *The Art and Science of Entrepreneurship*, Cambridge, Massachusetts: Ballinger, pp. 3-24.

Anderson, Poul H. (1995), *Collaborative Internationalisation of Small and Medium-Sized Enterprises*, Copenhagen: DJOF.

Auster, Ellen and Howard E. Aldrich (1984), "Small Business Vulnerability, Ethnic

Enclaves and Ethnic Enterprise," in Robin Ward and Richard Jenkins, eds., *Ethnic Communities in Business: Strategies for Economic Survival*, Cambridge: Cambridge University Press, pp. 39-54.

Bartlett, Christopher A. and Sumatra Ghoshal (1989), *Managing Across Borders: The Transnational Solution*, Boston: Harvard Business School Press.

Bilkey, Warren J. (1978), "An Attempted Integration of the Literature on the Export Behavior of Firms," *Journal of International Business Studies* 9(1), Spring/Summer, pp. 33-46.

Bilkey, Warren J. and George Tesar (1977), "The Export Behavior of Smaller Sized Wisconsin Manufacturing Firms," *Journal of International Business Studies* 8(1), Spring/Summer, pp. 93-98.

Boissevain, Jeremy and Hanneke Grotenbreg (1987), "Ethnic Enterprise in the Netherlands: The Surinamese of Amsterdam," in Robert Goffee and Robert Scase, eds., *Entrepreneurship in Europe: The Social Process*, London: Croom Helm, pp. 105-130.

Bonaccorsi, A. (1992), "On the Relationship Between Firm Size and Export Intensity," *Journal of International Business Studies* 23, pp. 605-635.

Brockhaus, Robert H., Sr. (1991), "Entrepreneurship, Education and Research Outside North America," *Entrepreneurship: Theory and Practice* 15(3), Spring, pp. 77-84.

Brush, Candida Greer (1995), *International Entrepreneurship: The Effect of Firm Age on Motives for Internationalisation*, New York: Garland.

Buckley, Peter J. (1997), "International Technology Transfer by Small and Medium-Sized Enterprises," *Small Business Economics* 9, pp. 67-78.

Buckley, Peter J. and Mark Casson (1976), *The Future of the Multinational Enterprise*, London: Macmillan.

Carsrud, Alan L., Connie Marie Gaglio and Kenneth W. Olm (1986), "Entrepreneurs–Mentors, Networks and Successful New Venture Development: An Exploratory Study," *Frontiers of Entrepreneurship Research*, Wellesley, Massachusetts: Babson College, pp. 229-243.

Carstairs, Robert T. and Lawrence S. Welch (1982), "Licensing and Internationalisation of Smaller Companies: Some Australian Evidence," *Management International Review* 22(3), pp. 33-44.

Caves, Richard E. (1971), "International Corporations: The Industrial Economics of Foreign Investment," *Economica*, February, pp. 1-27.

Cavusgil, S. Tamer (1980), "On the Internationalisation of Firms," *European Research* 8.

Cavusgil, S. Tamer (1984), "Differences Among Exporting Firms Based on Their Degree of Internationalisation," *Journal of Business Research* 12(2), pp. 195-208.

Cavusgil, S. Tamer, Warren J. Bilkey and George Tesar (1979), "A Note on the Export Behavior of Firms," *Journal of International Business Studies* 10(1), Spring/Summer, pp. 91-97.

Cavusgil, S. Tamer and V. Kirpalani (1993), "Introducing Products into Export Markets: Success Factors," *Journal of Business Research* 27(1), pp. 1-15.

Chen, Kuang-Jung (1997), "The Sari-Sari Store," *Journal of Small Business Management* 35(4), October, pp. 88-91.

Chen, Ming-Jer and Donald C. Hambrick (1995), "Speed, Stealth, and Selective Attack," *Academy of Management Journal* 38, pp. 453-482.

Contractor, Farok J. (1990), "Ownership Patterns of US Joint Ventures Abroad and the Liberalization of Foreign Government Regulations in the 1980s: Evidence from the Benchmark Surveys," *Journal of International Business Studies* 21(1), pp. 55-73.

Coviello, Nicole E. and H.J. Munro (1993), "Linkage Development and the Role of Marketing in the Internationalisation of the Entrepreneurial High Technology Firm," in G. Hills and R. W. LaForge and D.F. Muzyka, eds., *Research at Marketing/Entrepreneurship Interface,* Chicago: University of Chicago.

Cummings, Scott, ed. (1980), *Self-Help in Urban America: Patterns of Minority Business Enterprise,* Port Washington, New York: Kennikat, pp. 33-57.

Dana, Leo Paul (1987), "Entrepreneurship and Venture Creation–An International Comparison of Five Commonwealth Nations," *Frontiers of Entrepreneurship Research,* pp. 573-583.

Dana, Leo Paul (1990), "Saint Martin/Sint Maarten: A Case Study of the Effects of Politics and Culture on Economic Development," *Journal of Small Business Management* 28(4) October, pp. 91-98.

Dana, Leo Paul (1992), "A Look at Small Business in Austria," *Journal of Small Business Management* 30(4), October, pp. 126-130.

Dana, Leo Paul (1993), "An Analysis of Strategic Interventionist Policy in Namibia," *Journal of Small Business Management* 31(3), July, pp. 90-95

Dana, Leo Paul (1994), *Enterprising in the Global Environment,* Delhi: World Association for Small & Medium Enterprises.

Dana, Leo Paul (1995), "Entrepreneurship in a Remote Sub-Arctic Community," *Entrepreneurship, Theory and Practice,* 20(1), Fall, pp. 57-72.

Dana, Leo Paul (1997), "A Contrast of Argentina and Uruguay," *Journal of Small Business Management* 35(2), April, pp. 99-104.

Dana, Leo Paul (1998), "Waiting for Direction in the Former Yugoslav Republic of Macedonia," *Journal of Small Business Management* 36(2), April, pp. 62-67.

Dana, Leo Paul (1999), *Entrepreneurship in Pacific Asia: Past, Present & Future,* Singapore: World Scientific.

Dana, Leo Paul and Hamid Etemad (1994), "A Strategic Response Model for the Internationalisation of Small or Medium-Sized Australian Enterprises," *Bond Management Review* 4(1), September, pp. 31-42.

Dana, Leo Paul and Hamid Etemad (1995), "SMEs–Adapting Strategy for NAFTA: A Model for Small and Medium-Sized Enterprises," *Journal of Small Business & Entrepreneurship* 12(3), July-August, pp. 4-17.

Dichtl, Erwin, M. Leibold, Hans-Georg Köglmayr and Stefan Müller (1984), "The Export-Decision of Small and Medium-Sized Firms," *Management International Review* 24(2), pp. 49-60.

Dichtl, Erwin, M. Leibold, Hans-Georg Koeglmayr and Stefan Mueller (1990), "International Orientation as a Precondition for Export Success," *Journal of International Business Studies* 21(1), pp. 23-41.

Dubini, Paola and Howard E. Aldrich (1991), "Personal and Extended Networks Are

Central to the Entrepreneurship Process," *Journal of Business Venturing* 6(5), September, pp. 305-313.

Dunning, John H. (1973), "The Determinants of International Production," *Oxford Economic Papers*, November, pp. 289-336.

Dunning, John H. (1977), "Trade, Location of Economic Activity and MNEs: A Search for an Eclectic Approach," in *International Allocation of Economic Activity: Proceedings of a Nobel Symposium Held at Stockholm*, London: Macmillan, pp. 395-418.

Dunning, John H. (1980), "Toward an Eclectic Theory of International Production: Empirical Tests," *Journal of International Business Studies* 11(1), pp. 9-31.

Dunning, John H. (1988), "The Eclectic Paradigm of International Production: A Restatement and Some Possible Extensions," *Journal of International Business Studies*, 19(1), pp. 1-31.

Fan, Y., N. Chen and David A. Kirby (1996), "Chinese Peasant Entrepreneurs," *Journal of Small Business Management* 34(4), October, pp. 72-76.

Gadgil, Dhananjaya Ramchandra (1959), *Origins of the Modern Indian Business Class*, New York: Institute of Pacific Relations.

Geertz, Clifford (1963), *Peddlers and Princes: Social Development and Economic Change in Two Indonesian Towns*, Chicago, Illinois: University of Chicago Press.

Gibb, Allan A. (1986-7), "Education for Enterprise," *Journal of Small Business & Entrepreneurship* 4(3), Winter, pp. 42-48.

Golden, P. A. and M. Dollinger (1993), "Co-operative Alliance and Competitive Strategies in Small Manufacturing Firms," *Entrepreneurship: Theory and Practice*, Summer, pp. 43-56.

Grabinsky, Salo (1996), "Crisis in Mexico: Its Effects on Family Owned Businesses," *Journal of Enterprising Culture* 4(3), September, pp. 301-316.

Harrison, Bennett (1997), *Lean and Mean*, New York: Gilford.

Hazlehurst, Leighton W. (1966), *Entrepreneurship and the Merchant Castes in a Punjabi City*, Durham, North Carolina: Duke University Commonwealth Studies Center.

Hisrich, Robert D. and Guyula Fulop (1995), "Hungarian Entrepreneurs and Their Enterprises," *Journal of Small Business Management* 33(3), July, pp. 88-94.

Hisrich, Robert D. and Janos Vecsenyi (1990), "Entrepreneurship and the Hungarian Transformation," *Journal of Managerial Psychology* 5(5), pp. 11-16.

Holmquist, Carin and Elisabeth Sundin (1988), "Women as Entrepreneurs in Sweden–Conclusions from a Survey," *Frontiers of Entrepreneurship Research*, pp. 626-642.

Hymer, Stephan (1976), *The International Operations of National Firms: A Study of Direct Foreign Investment*, Cambridge, Massachusetts: MIT Press.

Johanson, Jan and Associates (1994), *Internationalisation, Relationships and Networks*, Stockholm: Almquist & Wiksell International.

Johanson, Jan and Jan-Erik Vahlne (1977), "The Internationalization Process of the Firm–A Model of Knowledge Development and Increasing Foreign Market Commitments," *Journal of International Business Studies* 8(1), Spring/Summer, pp. 23-32.

Johanson, Jan and Finn Wiedersheim-Paul (1975), "The Internationalisation of the

Firm: Four Swedish Cases," *Journal of International Management Studies* 12(3), October, pp. 305-322.

Knickerbocker, Frederick T. (1973), *Oligopolistic Reaction and Multinational Enterprise*, Cambridge: Division of Research, Graduate School of Business Administration, Harvard University.

Larson, A. (1991), "Partner Networks," *Journal of Business Venturing* 6, pp. 173-188.

Light, Ivan (1972), *Ethnic Enterprise in America: Business and Welfare Among Chinese, Japanese and Blacks*, Berkeley, California: University of California.

Light, Ivan (1984), "Immigrant and Ethnic Enterprise in North America," *Ethnic and Racial Studies*, 7(2), pp. 195-216.

Light, Ivan and Edna Bonacich (1988), *Immigrant Entrepreneurs: Koreans in Los Angeles 1965-1985*, Berkeley, California: University of California Press.

Lipparini, A. and M. Sobrero (1994), "The Glue and the Pieces," *Journal of Business Venturing* 9, pp. 125-140.

Liuhto, Kari (1996), "The Transformation of the Enterprise Sector in Estonia," *Journal of Enterprising Culture* 4(3), September, pp. 317-329.

Martin, James H. and Bruno Grbac (1998), "Small and Large Firms' Marketing Activities as a Response to Economic Privatization," *Journal of Small Business Management* 36(1), January, pp. 95-99.

McGee, J.E. and M.J. Dowling (1994), "Using R&D Co-operative Agreements to Leverage Managerial Experience," *Journal of Business Venturing* 9(1), pp. 33-48.

Min, Pyong Gap and Charles Jaret (1985), "Ethnic Business Success: The Case of Korean Small Business in Atlanta," *Sociology and Social Research* 69(3), April, pp. 412-435.

Morita, Keiko and John C. Oliga (1991), "Collective Global Entrepreneurship," in John C. Oliga and T.B. Kim, eds., *Proceedings of the ENDEC World Conference on Entrepreneurship and Innovative Change*, Singapore: Nanyang Technological University, pp. 450-451.

Newbould, G.D., Peter J. Buckley and J.C. Thurwell (1978), *Going International–The Enterprise of Smaller Companies Overseas,* New York: John Wiley and Sons.

Noar, Jacob (1985), "Recent Small Business Reforms in Hungary," *Journal of Small Business Management* 23(1), January, pp. 65-72.

Ojuka-Onedo, A.E. (1996), "Interventionist Policy in Enterprise Development Using the Rural Poor in Agrarian Developing Countries," *Entrepreneurship, Innovation, and Change* 5(3), September, pp. 263-265.

Oviatt, Benjamin Milton and Patricia Phillips McDougall (1994), "Toward a Theory of International New Ventures," *Journal of International Business Studies* 25(1), pp. 45-64.

Pache, Gilles (1996), "The Small Producer in the French Food Distribution Channel," *Journal of Small Business Management* 34(2), April, pp. 84-88.

Patel, V.G. (1987), *Entrepreneurship Development Programme in India and Its Relevance to Developing Countries*, Ahmedabad: Entrepreneurship Development Institute of India.

Raghunanda, M. (1995), "Entrepreneurial Survival Skills in the Midst of Economic Chaos," *Journal of Enterprising Culture* 3(4), December, pp. 463-482.

Reynolds, Paul D. (1997), "New and Small Firms in Expanding Markets," *Small Business Economics* 9, pp. 79-84.

Sarder, Jahangir H., Dipak Ghosh and Peter Rosa (1997), "The Importance of Support Services to Small Firms in Bangladesh," *Journal of Small Business Management* 35(2), April, pp. 26-36.

Schumpeter, Joseph Allois (1911), *Theorie der wirtschaftlichen Entwicklung, Munich and Leipzig: Dunker und Humblat*; translated (1934) by R. Opie, *The Theory of Economic Development*, Cambridge, Massachusetts: Harvard University Press.

Shepherd, J. (1991), "Entrepreneurial Growth Through Constellations," *Journal of Business Venturing* 6, pp. 363-373.

Sherman, Andrew J. (1996), "International Franchising: Strategies for Building Bridges Between Asia and North America," *Journal of International Business & Entrepreneurship* 4(1) pp. 1-28.

Silva-Castan, Jaime R., Luis Prott and Servulo Anzola-Rojas (1997), "An Innovative Program in Entrepreneurship Development at a Mexican University," *Journal of Enterprising Culture* 5(1), March, pp. 1-12.

Simon, Hermann (1992), "Lessons from Germany's Midsize Giants," *Harvard Business Review* 70 (2), pp. 115-123.

Tallman, S.B. and Oded Shenkar (1994), "A Managerial Decision Model of International Co-operative Venture Foundings," *Journal of International Business Studies* 25, pp. 91-113.

Tambunan, Tulus (1992), "The Role of Small Firms in Indonesia," *Small Business Economics* 4(1), March, pp. 59-77.

Tesar, George and J.S. Tarleton (1982), "Comparison of Wisconsin and Virginia Small and Medium Sized Exporters: Aggressive and Passive Exporters," in Michael R. Czinkota and George Tesar, eds., *Export Management: An International Context*, New York, pp. 85-112.

Vernon, Raymond (1966), "International Investment and International Trade and the Product Cycle," *Quarterly Journal of Economics*, May, pp. 190-207.

Vernon, Raymond (1979), "The Product Cycle Hypothesis in a New International Environment," *Oxford Bulletin of Economics and Statistics* 41, November, pp. 255-267.

Walsh, James and Philip Anderson (1995), "Owner-Manager Adoption/Innovation Preference and Employment Performance," *Journal of Small Business Management* 33(3), July, pp. 1-8.

Ward, Robin (1987), "Ethnic Entrepreneurs in Britain and in Europe," in R. Scase and R. Goffee, eds., *Entrepreneurship in Europe*, London: Croom Helm, pp. 83-104.

Ward, Robin and Richard Jenkins, eds. (1984), *Ethnic Communities in Business: Strategies for Economic Survival*, Cambridge: Cambridge University Press, pp. 105-124.

Welch, Lawrence S. (1992), "The Use of Alliances by Small Firms in Achieving Internationalisation," *Scandinavian International Business Review* 1(2), pp. 21-37.

Wimalatissa, W.A. (1996), "The Emerging Class of Businesswomen and Women-Owned Business Firms in Brunei Darussalem," *Journal of Enterprising Culture* 4(3), September, pp. 287-300.

Wong, Bernard (1987), "The Role of Ethnicity in Enclave Enterprises: A Study of the Chinese Garment Factories in New York City," *Human Organisation* 66(2), Summer, pp. 120-130.

Wright, Richard W. (1989), "Networking, Japanese Style," *Business Quarterly*, 54 (2) Autumn, pp. 20-24.

Wu, Yuan Li (1983), "The Role of Alien Entrepreneurs in Economic Development: An Entrepreneurial Problem," *American Economic Review* 73(2), May, pp. 112-117.

An Integrative Conceptual Model

Bostjan Antoncic
Robert D. Hisrich

SUMMARY. International entrepreneurship is an emerging research area. It seems to be divided into two main research streams: a traditional area of SME internationalisation and an emerging area of international start-ups. Our study attempts to integrate the two streams by proposing an integrative conceptual model of international entrepreneurship. The model is built around the concept of internationalisation that consists of internationalisation properties (time and mode) and internationalisation performance. Other building blocks of the model are internationalisation antecedents (environmental conditions and organisational characteristics) and internationalisation consequences (organisational performance). A set of propositions about relationships in the conceptual model is developed and implications are proposed. *[Article copies available for a fee from The Haworth Document Delivery Service: 1-800-342-9678. E-mail address: <getinfo@haworthpressinc.com> Website: <http://www.HaworthPress.com>]*

KEYWORDS. Internationalisation, SMEs, start-ups, international entrepreneurship

INTRODUCTION

International entrepreneurship is an emerging research field at the interface of entrepreneurship and international business research. Its

Bostjan Antoncic and Robert D. Hisrich are both affiliated with Case Western Reserve University, USA.

[Haworth co-indexing entry note]: "An Integrative Conceptual Model." Antoncic, Bostjan, and Robert D. Hisrich. Co-published simultaneously in *Journal of Euromarketing* (International Business Press, an imprint of The Haworth Press, Inc.) Vol. 9, No. 2, 2000, pp. 17-35; and: *Global Marketing Co-Operation and Networks* (ed: Leo Paul Dana) International Business Press, an imprint of The Haworth Press, Inc., 2000, pp. 17-35. Single or multiple copies of this article are available for a fee from The Haworth Document Delivery Service [1-800-342-9678, 9:00 a.m. - 5:00 p.m. (EST). E-mail address: getinfo@haworthpress inc.com].

importance has been increasing due in part to increased globalisation and hyper-competition. In addition to the long tradition in small business internationalisation research, the last decade has witnessed the emergence of a new entrepreneurial research area of international new ventures (McDougall, 1989; McDougall, Shane and Oviatt, 1994; Oviatt and McDougall, 1994, 1997). Although systematic reviews of international entrepreneurship exist (McDougall and Oviatt, 1997; Dana, Etemad and Wright, 1998), there is still a lack of an integrative theory of international entrepreneurship.

To date, research in this area can be divided into two main research streams: (1) Small & Medium Entreprise (SME) internationalisation and (2) international start-ups. International entrepreneurship can be best understood when both are considered. By integrating the two research streams a more comprehensive model of international entrepreneurship can be built. This paper focuses on building a theory of international entrepreneurship instead of building partial theories of SME export performance (Holzmuller and Kasper, 1991) or international new ventures (Oviatt and McDougall, 1994). First, the domain of international entrepreneurship and two key research streams (SME internationalisation and international start-ups) are discussed. Then, a model of international entrepreneurship, which includes a concept of internationalisation and its antecedents (environmental conditions and organisational characteristics) and consequences (firm performance), is developed and its implications are proposed.

DOMAIN OF INTERNATIONAL ENTREPRENEURSHIP

In a recent review, McDougall and Oviatt defined the area of international entrepreneurship as: "International entrepreneurship is defined as new and innovative activities that have the goal of value creation and growth in business organisations across national borders ... international entrepreneurship concerns value creation and growth activities that span national borders, and cross-border comparisons of domestic business activities" (1997, pp. 293). In this definition, the authors included both internationalisation issues of entrepreneurs and cross-cultural comparisons of entrepreneurship issues under the domain of international entrepreneurship. While a workable definition, it is still too broad as cross-cultural or cross-national entrepreneurship research should be considered as a research area that is separate from research on internationalisation of entrepreneurs. Cross-cultural research is aimed at understanding how things are done in different cultures or nations, and improving the understanding of theories and assessing their generalisability across different systems of meaning, belief and action (Earley and Singh, 1995). It has the potential to expand concepts and theories developed in a single cultural setting (Brislin, 1980) and form a basis for assessment of universal laws on relationships between variables (Triandis, 1980). Cross-cultural research deals with various entrepreneurship issues and compares them across different cultures. In contrast, in international entrepreneurship the research focus should be on internationalisation issues. Only cross-cultural entrepreneurship research that focuses on cross-cultural comparisons of internationalisation issues should be included in the domain of international entrepreneurship. Or, alternatively, this research area might be named internationalisation entrepreneurship.

International entrepreneurship is a part of entrepreneurship research which has a domain that includes issues related to formation, transformation and growth of firms. International entrepreneurship shares commonalties with international business research and focuses on various internationalisation issues, such as exporting and other entry modes, economic development initiatives, venture financing, international new ventures, and co-operative alliances (McDougall and Oviatt, 1997). Historically, there have been two main research streams in international entrepreneurship: (1) small business internationalisation and (2) international start-ups.

Small Business Internationalisation

Research in small business internationalisation has always been central to international entrepreneurship. In the last decade there has been continuing interest in research in this area, especially in exporting and other entry modes (McDougall and Oviatt, 1997). Internationalisation is important for different countries because of its benefits such as its impact on economic growth (Jaffe and Pasternak, 1994), and on a country's well being and international reputation (Dichtl, Koeglmayr and Mueller, 1990). Special attention in this area has been given to the export performance, predominantly in terms of such correlates as: firm size (Culpan, 1989; Walters and Samiee, 1990; Ali and Swiercz, 1991; Agarwal and Ramaswami, 1992; Bonaccorsi, 1992; Erramilli and D'Souza, 1993; Berra, Piatti and Vitali, 1995; Kohn,

1997), firm age (Nakos, Brouthers and Brouthers, 1998), strategy (Baird, Lyles and Orris, 1994; Tybee, 1994), perceptions (Jaffe and Pasternak, 1994), orientations (Dichtl, Koeglmayr and Mueller, 1994), international experience (Reuber and Fischer, 1997), attitudes (Donthu and Kim, 1993; Bijmolt and Zwart, 1994; Ogbuehi and Longfellow, 1994), commitment (Donthu and Kim, 1993; Cavusgil and Kirpalani, 1993) and other characteristics of managers (Nakos, Brouthers and Brouthers, 1998), organisation characteristics and organisation culture (Holzmuller and Kasper, 1991), product characteristics (Beamish, Craig and McLellan, 1993; Katsikeas, Deng and Wortzel, 1997), distribution and marketing focus characteristics (Beamish, Craig and McLellan, 1993), and industry environment (Tybee, 1994).

Other issues in the area of small business internationalisation have been: the role of networks for internationalisation (Hara and Kanai, 1994; Coviello and Munro, 1995; Zafarullah, Ali and Young, 1998), international joint ventures (D'Souza and McDougall, 1989; Barrett, 1992; Au and Enderwick, 1994) and alliances (Welch, 1992; Hansen, Gillespie and Gencturk, 1994), export information (Cafferata and Mensi, 1995; McDowell and Rowlands, 1995; Chaudhry and Crick, 1998), relationships with suppliers (Jones and Kustin, 1995), international channel choice decisions (Ramaseshan and Patton, 1994), governmental export policies and programmes (Terpstra and Yu, 1992; Czinkota, 1994; Ghauri and Herbern, 1994; Levie, 1994; Korhonen, Luostarinen and Welch, 1996; Moini, 1998; Weaver, Berkowitz and Davies, 1998), international transfer of technology (Balachandra, 1996; Buckley, 1997), innovativeness (Boter and Holmquist, 1996) and diffusion of innovations (Acs, Morck, Shaver and Yeung, 1997), export stimuli (Caughey and Chetty, 1994), personal and personnel adjustments (Wright, 1993), and export financing (Tannous and Sarkar, 1993). As is indicated, the research area of small business internationalisation is broad and includes a variety of research issues. Inclusion of cross-cultural domestic research on small businesses in this area would unnecessarily extend its domain and lessen its internationalisation focus.

Overall, in this research area the internationalisation processes of firms have been predominantly viewed as incremental, following the stage theory of internationalisation (Johanson and Wiedersheim-Paul, 1975; Bilkey and Tesar, 1977; Johanson and Vahlne, 1977; Cavusgil 1984; Bartlett and Ghoshal, 1989). Internationalisation, according to this approach, evolves incrementally through stages from less to more complex modes of organisational international activity. A firm's international activities would typically start with indirect exporting or importing and evolve through direct exporting or importing to more progressive stages (licensing, joint ventures, and wholly-owned subsidiaries). Congruently according to stage theory, export involvement can be seen as incremental. Regardless of firm size, due to increased export experience, the degree of export involvement can be viewed as evolving. For example, it was proposed that exporting progresses through five stages (Daniels and Radebaugh, 1994): (1) partial interest in exporting, (2) exploring exporting, (3) experimental exporter, (4) experienced exporter with limited scope, and (5) experienced exporter. Even though stage theory has been a dominant approach to internationalisation in entrepreneurship in the last two decades, another research stream, that revealed evidence of the limitations of stage models, emerged in the last decade; this has been labelled international start-ups.

International Start-Ups

This research stream has revealed that many firms do not follow the traditional pattern of internationalisation proposed by stage theory. Some firms are international from their birth. Some international start-ups have been called: international new ventures (McDougall, 1989; McDougall, Shane and Oviatt, 1994; Oviatt and McDougall, 1994, 1997), born globals (Madsen and Servais, 1997), and global start-ups (Oviatt and McDougall, 1995). Factors, which influence firms to internationalise from their inception, may have very similar roots as factors that influence internationalisation of small- and medium-sized firms. In the case of international start-ups such factors are (1) industry characteristics (McDougall, 1989), and (2) characteristics of founders, such as: their knowledge and background (McDougall, Shane and Oviatt, 1994), international experience (Madsen and Servais, 1997), network of business alliances (Coviello and Munro, 1992; Oviatt, McDougall, Simon and Shrader, 1993; McDougall, Shane and Oviatt, 1994), strategy (McDougall, 1989), and attitude and philosophy (McDougall, Shane and Oviatt, 1994). While the separation of international start-ups from small business internationalisation is based on arguments about the specificity of the time of internationalisation, in terms of internationalisation correlates, it is somewhat arbitrary at best.

Indeed, according to Madsen and Servais (1997), the international start-up does not represent any revolutionary pattern of internationalisation but rather it may be viewed in the evolutionary framework by extending its time perspective beyond its inception, since it has roots in founders and top managers' industry experience that was gained in previous firms and networks. Bloodgood, Sapienza and Almeida (1997) argued that the stage theory of internationalisation includes useful elements to understand international start-ups, such as the use of advantages, knowledge and experience.

Based on this previous research, this study proposes an integrative conceptual model of internationalisation. In the model, international start-ups are differentiated from small business internationalisation by the time of internationalisation, but both share common antecedents and consequences.

A CONCEPTUAL MODEL

In this section the key concepts of international entrepreneurship (internationalisation and its antecedents and consequences) are discussed and a set of propositions that build a model of international entrepreneurship is developed.

Internationalisation

The concept of internationalisation is basically constructed from internationalisation properties (time and mode) and internationalisation performance.

Internationalisation Properties

Time and mode of internationalisation are two key internationalisation properties. Internationalisation time is a crucial property because it links together internationalisation research on SMEs that are international from inception and those that internationalise later in the life of the firm. Early internationalisation (Oviatt and McDougall, 1994) can be seen as an internationalisation characteristic that separates international new ventures from internationalisation of SMEs. When a firm enters a foreign market early and its decision to extend its international operations is based on previous experience and structure (path dependency), then the time of entry is a defining factor of SME internationalisation.

The delay after start-up in obtaining foreign sales can also be considered a measure of international behaviour (Reuber and Fischer, 1997). There is a question about what should constitute a cut-off point in international involvement that would indicate the beginning of actual internationalisation. In previous research, different thresholds of export intensity, such as 5% (McDougall, 1989) and 10% (Dichtl, Koeglmayr and Mueller, 1990) have been proposed for classification of a firm as being international or domestic. Despite this arbitrariness in defining the exact time of the beginning of internationalisation, the time of internationalisation is an important internationalisation property.

The second property is the mode of internationalisation. Four most commonly used foreign entry modes, according to Agarwal and Ramaswami (1992), that are distinguished in their foreign investment intensiveness are exporting, licensing, joint venture and sole venture. The least involved mode is exporting. It is "an attractive foreign-market entry mode for many firms due to the lower commitment requirements of company resources involved in exporting, as contrasted with alternative types of international operations, such as joint ventures and overseas operations" (Katsikaes, 1994, p. 33). The mode of internationalisation refers to the intensity of involvement in international operations in terms of foreign investment intensiveness that ranges from no involvement to totally-owned firms.

Internationalisation Performance

Internationalisation performance mainly refers to the extent and growth of international sales. The two most frequently used export performance criteria are export intensity (percentage of sales accounted for by export) and export sales growth (Aaby and Slater, 1989; Walters and Samie, 1990; Moini, 1995). Other indicators of export performance are export sales profitability in comparison to domestic sales profitability (Bijmolt and Zwart, 1994; Nakos, Brouthers and Brouthers, 1998), geographic scope of foreign sales (Culpan, 1989; Reuber and Fischer, 1997) and management satisfaction with export performance (Bijmolt and Zwart, 1994). Internationalisation performance is an important outcome of internationalisation. Under the international new ventures theory it is primarily influenced by the time of internationalisation, whereas under stage theory it would progress incrementally along with the evolution from less to more complex modes of organisational internationalisation activity. Therefore, it can be expected that internationalisation performance will be influenced by internationalisation properties. This leads to the following proposition:

> *Proposition 1:* Internationalisation properties (time and mode) will be associated with internationalisation performance.

Antecedents of Internationalisation

Environmental conditions and organisational characteristics can be viewed as key antecedents of internationalisation.

Environmental Conditions

Four environmental conditions are extremely important for internationalisation. These are characteristics of the domestic market, characteristics of foreign markets, market internationalisation, and industry.

The characteristics of the domestic market, such as size, degree of immigrants and internal competitiveness can influence internationalisation. Madsen and Servais (1997) proposed that nations with small domestic markets and high percentage of immigrants could be associated with higher number of international start-ups. Exporting can be vitally important for small countries with open economies (Bijmolt and Zwart, 1994). Bloodgood, Sapienza and Almeida (1997) found that domestic industry profitability could be negatively associated with internationalisation of newer small US firms. Indeed, highly competitive domestic market conditions may influence internationalisation (Nakos, Brouthers and Brouthers, 1998). Thus, it can be expected that domestic markets that are relatively larger, more internally competitive and have more immigrants will positively impact internationalisation.

Second, characteristics of the foreign markets, such as market proximity, potential and country-specific investment risk can influence internationalisation. An important environmental factor is proximity to the export market (Madsen, 1989) in terms of geographic as well as cultural distance (Calof and Viviers, 1995). Two other characteristics that may influence not only choice of whether to enter but also the choice of mode of entry are market potential (size and growth) and investment risk that may adversely affect both the entry and the investment entry mode (Agarwal and Ramaswami, 1992). It is expected that foreign markets that are relatively more proximate, have relatively larger potential and relatively lower country-specific investment risk will have a positive impact on internationalisation.

Third, the environmental condition that may influence SME internationalisation is market internationalisation. Speed of internationalisation may be much higher in internationalised market conditions (Johanson and Mattsson, 1988). In fact, internationalised markets may be a necessary condition for international start-ups (Madsen and Servais, 1997). Therefore, it can be expected that market internationalisation will have a positive impact on firm internationalisation.

Fourth, the industry in which a firm competes may influence its internationalisation. Moini (1995) emphasised the need to explore export behaviour on an industry-by-industry basis because firms in different industries may differ in their export behaviour. Technology intensiveness can be related to the propensity to export (Aaby and Slater, 1989). Early internationalisation is particularly important for firms in knowledge-based industries such as software industry (Oviatt and McDougall, 1994). Bonaccorsi (1992) and Reuber and Fischer (1997) also argued that industry-specific characteristics could affect SME internationalisation. Thus, it is expected that the industry will have an impact on internationalisation. This research leads to the following proposition:

> *Proposition 2:* Environmental conditions (characteristics of the domestic market, characteristics of foreign markets, market internationalisation and industry) will be associated with internationalisation properties and performance.

Organisational Characteristics

A second set of factors that can influence internationalisation are organisational characteristics. These are firm size, strategy, international experience, international orientation, networking and other founders/managers' and firm characteristics.

First, firm size can influence internationalisation. Larger firms may be more internationalised than smaller firms because they: (1) possess more financial and managerial resources; (2) have greater production capacity; (3) attain higher levels of economies of scale; and (4) are more likely to be associated with lower levels of perceived risk in exporting operations (Bonaccorsi, 1992). A higher extent of internationalisation of larger relative to smaller SMEs was found for US high-potential ventures (Bloodgood, Sapienza and Almeida, 1997) and for Pennsylvania (Culpan, 1989) and Wisconsin manufacturing firms (Moini, 1995). Nakos, Brouthers and Brouthers (1998) found that larger Greek SMEs had higher export performance than smaller firms. Exporting manufacturing firms tended to be larger than non-exporting firms in terms of workforce and sales volume (Keng and Jiuan, 1989). Larger firms, in contrast to smaller ones, enjoy more competitive advantages in export markets (Katsikeas, 1994). In addition, larger firms may have higher propensity to choose sole and joint venture internationalisation modes (Agarwal and Ramaswami, 1992). Therefore, even if the effect of firm size was not found in some countries with small domestic markets (Bonaccorsi, 1992; Reuber and Fischer, 1997), firm size will be positively related with internationalisation.

Second, strategy can influence internationalisation. Product and market differentiation strategies have been found to be positively related to internationalisation (Bloodgood, Sapienza and Almeida, 1997). Strategy formulation in terms of systematically exploring, analysing, and planning for export can be crucial for successful exporting (Aaby and Slater, 1989; Bijmolt and Zwart, 1994). Successful exporters tend to systematically explore export possibilities more than do less successful ones (Moini, 1995). In addition, internationalisation mode selection is often based on strategy considerations, or in other words, it is basically a critical strategic decision (Agarwal and Ramaswami, 1992). Therefore, it can be expected that strategy will impact internationalisation.

Third, international experience can influence internationalisation. Nakos, Brouthers and Brouthers (1998) found a positive relationship between international experience of Greek SME managers and export performance in terms of export intensity and export sales profitability in comparison to domestic sales profitability. Bloodgood, Sapienza and Almeida (1997) found a positive relationship between international work experience of managers, but not international schooling, and the extent of internationalisation at the time of the initial public offering of newer high-potential firms. Strong international experience of the entrepreneur can be viewed as an antecedent of an international start-up (Madsen and Servais, 1997) and SME internationalisation in terms of internationalisation time and intensity (Reuber and Fischer, 1997). In addition, any delay in obtaining foreign sales was found to mediate the international experience-international intensity relationship of Canadian software SMEs (Reuber and Fischer, 1997). International experience can be seen as crucial for exporting success (Aaby and Slater, 1989; Katsikaes, 1994) and successful exporters tend to visit foreign markets more frequently than less successful ones (Moini, 1995). International experience may also influence internationalisation mode choice since less experienced firms may be more likely to select non-investment modes such as exporting (Agarwal and Ramaswami, 1992). This research indicates that international experience will positively impact internationalisation.

Fourth, international orientation can influence internationalisation. Commitment to international operations was found to be positively related to export performance (Walters and Samie, 1990; Nakos, Brouthers and Brouthers, 1998). Management commitment to internationalisation, attitudes, perceptions and expectations tends to be positively related to propensity to export (Aaby and Slater, 1989; Bijmolt and Zwart, 1994; Moini, 1995). This indicates that international orientation will positively impact internationalisation.

Fifth, organisational as well as personal networks can be seen as an additional important element for internationalisation. Madsen and Servais (1997) emphasised that the internationalisation process of the individual firm cannot be viewed in isolation, but should be understood by analysing the firm's inter-organisational relationships. Johanson and Mattsson (1988) considered the firm's relationships in industrial networks as an important element in the internationalisation process. Hara and Kanai (1994) considered international strategic alliances among small businesses as important vehicles for their success. Personal networks of founders from their previous involvement in international marketing were crucial in international new venture creation (Hansen and Witkowski, 1995). Coviello and Munro (1992), exploring the internationalisation and growth through linkage development, found the process became more sophisticated and formalised as the managers gained more experience with linkage relationships and international markets. Similarly, Coviello and Munro (1995) focused on the impact of network relationships on international market development and on marketing-related activities within international markets. They found that the interests of other players in the network of relationships shape internationalisation efforts, and that relationships were established to compensate for limited marketing expertise and infrastructure. It is expected that personal and organisational networking will be positively related to internationalisation.

Other characteristics of founders/managers can also influence internationalisation. These include such demographics of founders/managers as: age (Holzmuller and Kasper, 1991; Moini, 1995; Nakos, Brouthers and Brouthers, 1998), education level (Holzmuller and Kasper, 1991; Moini, 1995; Keng and Jiuan, 1989), and foreign language fluency (Aaby and Slater, 1989; Dichtl, Koeglmayr and Mueller, 1990; Holzmuller and Kasper, 1991; Moini, 1995; Nakos, Brouthers and Brouthers, 1998). Additional firm characteristics that can impact internationalisation are firm age (Holzmuller and Kasper, 1991; Reuber and Fischer, 1997; Nakos, Brouthers and Brouthers, 1998), trained export personnel (Nakos, Brouthers and Brouthers, 1998), foreign ownership (Keng and Jiuan, 1989; Nakos, Brouthers and Brouthers, 1998) and organisational culture (Holzmuller and Kasper, 1991). All these findings from previous research lead to the following proposition:

> *Proposition 3:* Organisational characteristics (firm size, strategy, international experience, international orientation, networking and other founders/managers' and firm characteristics) are related to internationalisation properties and performance.

Consequences of Internationalisation

Organisational performance in terms of growth and profitability is the ultimate result indicating whether internationalisation ultimately does pay. The extent of foreign operations may be related to organisational performance as a firm can use interrelationships between different market segments, related industries and geographical areas by exploiting economies of scale, scope and experience (Kogut, 1985; Porter, 1985; Riahi-Belkaoui, 1998). While the growth of firms is central to the domain of international entrepreneurship (Giamartino, McDougall and Bird, 1993; McDougall and Oviatt, 1997), empirical evidence for this relationship is minimal. Bloodgood, Sapienza and Almeida (1997) found a positive but not significant relationship between the extent of internationalisation and sales growth. Despite this fact, both SME internationalisation and international new ventures literature seem to recognise the relationship between internationalisation performance and firm growth. Therefore, it can be expected that internationalisation performance will have a positive impact on firm growth, the essence of the following proposition:

> *Proposition 4:* Internationalisation performance will be positively associated with firm growth.

Effects of internationalisation on profitability have been criticised as inconclusive and inconsistent (Sullivan, 1994; Riahi-Belkaoui, 1998). This may reflect, in part, the non-linearity of the internationalisation-profitability relationship. Riahi-Belkaui (1998) found non-monotonic relationship between the degree of internationalisation and the rate of return on assets (ROA). His results based on a cross-sectional study of 100 American firms indicated that with increasing internationalisation the relationship is first negative, then positive and finally negative. Therefore, a reversed-U-shaped functional relationship between internationalisation performance and profitability is expected as is indicated in the following proposition:

> *Proposition 5:* The association between internationalisation performance and profitability will be non-linear (reversed-U-shape).

CONCLUSIONS AND IMPLICATIONS

International entrepreneurship is an important emerging research area that is lacking any comprehensive theory. This study contributes to theory development by developing a model of international entrepreneurship that links the two main steams of research (SME internationalisation and international new ventures). The resulting integrative model of SME internationalisation is centred on the concept of internationalisation that includes internationalisation time, internationalisation mode and internationalisation performance. The model contains also key antecedents (environmental conditions and organisational characteristics) and consequences (firm performance) of internationalisation.

Some limitations of the proposed contingency model need to be noted. The model of internationalisation is comprehensive but not exhaustive as it incorporates the most important antecedents and consequences of internationalisation. In addition, it does not specifically address interactions among constructs. An example of research that points to the inclusion of interaction effects is the study of Agarwal and Ramaswami (1992) based on the US equipment industry. The authors found that the choice of entry mode can result from interactions among different elements, such as interaction among firm size, experience and market potential and between product differentiation strategy, and market potential, and market associated risks. In future research interaction effects should be studied in addition to the main effects among the constructs presented in this initial international entrepreneurship model.

In-depth case studies and longitudinal research designs may offer most valuable insights in this research area. First, the proposed model can be used as an overall conceptual framework for conducting in-depth comparative case studies. In this way processes of internationalisation can be better understood. Second, longitudinal research designs are essential because time lags may exist in assessing the impacts of environmental conditions and organisational characteristics on internationalisation; internationalisation properties on internationalisation performance; and internationalisation performance on firm performance. In addition, cross-national comparative studies should be conducted to assess generalisability of the model.

An important implication of the model for practitioners is that they should be aware of the complexity of internationalisation and the need to constantly evaluate multiple elements related to SME internationalisation. The proposed model provides a framework that can be used in designing firm-specific, customised models of internationalisation.

REFERENCES

Aaby, N. and S.F. Slater (1989), "Management Influences on Export Performance: A Review of the Empirical Literature 1978-88," *International Marketing Review* 6(4), pp. 7-26.

Acs, Z.J., R. Morck, J.M. Shaver and B. Yeung (1997), "The Internationalization of Small and Medium-sized Enterprises: A Policy Perspective," *Small Business Economics* 9(1), pp. 7-20.

Agarwal, S. and S.N. Ramaswami (1992), "Choice of Foreign Market Entry Mode: Impact of Ownership, Location and Internalization Focus," *Journal of International Business Studies* 23, pp. 1-27.

Ali, A. and P.M. Swiercz (1991), "Firm Size and Export Behavior: Lessons from the Midwest," *Journal of Small Business Management* 29(2), pp. 71-78.

Au, Kai Ming and P. Enderwick (1994), "Small Firms in International Joint Ventures in China: The New Zealand Experience," *Journal of Small Business Management* 32(2), pp. 88-94.

Baird, I.S., M.A. Lyles and J.B. Orris (1994), "The Choice of International Strategies by Small Businesses," *Journal of Small Business Management* 32(1), pp. 48-59.

Balachandra, R. (1996), "International Technology Transfer in Small Business: A New Paradigm," *International Journal of Technology Management* 12(5,6), pp. 625-638.

Barrett, G.R. (1992), "Finding the Right International Partner for Small Businesses," *Journal of Accountancy* 173(1), pp. 58-64.

Bartlett, C.A. and S. Ghoshal (1989), *Managing Across Borders: The Transnational Solution*, Boston, Massachusetts: Harvard Business School Press.

Beamish, P.W., R. Craig and K. McLellan (1993), "The Performance Characteristics of Canadian versus U.K. Exporters in Small and Medium Sized Firms," *Management International Review* 33(2), pp. 121-137.

Berra, L., L. Piatti and G.Vitali (1995), "The Internationalisation Process in the Small and Medium Sized Firms: A Case Study on the Italian Clothing Industry," *Small Business Economics* 7(1), pp. 67-75.

Bijmolt, T.H.A. and P.S. Zwart (1994), "The Impact of Internal Factors on the Export Success of Dutch Small and Medium-sized Firms," *Journal of Small Business Management* 32(2), pp. 69-83.

Bilkey, W.J. and G. Tesar (1977), "The Export Behavior of Smaller Sized Wisconsin Manufacturing Firms," *Journal of International Business Studies* 8(1), pp. 33-46.

Bloodgood, J.M., H.J. Sapienza and J.G. Almeida (1997), "The Internationalisation of New High-potential U.S. Ventures: Antecedents and Outcomes," *Entrepreneurship: Theory and Practice* 20(4), pp. 61-76.

Bonaccorsi, A. (1992), "On the Relationship Between Firm Size and Export Intensity," *Journal of International Business Studies* 23(4), pp. 605-635.

Boter, H. and C. Holmquist (1996), "Industry Characteristics and Internationalisation Processes in Small Firms," *Journal of Business Venturing* 11(6), pp. 471-487.

Brislin, R.W. (1980), "Introduction," in H. C. Triandis and R.W. Brislin, eds., *Handbook of Cross-cultural Psychology, Vol. 5, Social Psychology*, Boston, Massachusetts: Allyn and Bacon, pp. 1-24.

Buckley, P.J. (1997), "International Technology Transfer by Small and Medium-sized Enterprises," *Small Business Economics* 9(1), pp. 67-78.

Cafferata, R. and R. Mensi (1995), "The Role of Information in the Internationalisation of SMEs: A Typological Approach," *International Small Business Journal* 13(3), pp. 35-46.

Calof, J.L. and W. Viviers (1995), "Internationalisation Behaviour of Small- and Medium-sized South African Enterprises," *Journal of Small Business Management* 33(4), pp. 71-79.

Caughey, M. and S. Chetty (1994), "Pre-export Behaviour of Small Manufacturing Firms in New Zealand," *International Small Business Journal* 12(3), pp. 62-68.

Cavusgil, S.T. (1984), "Differences Among Exporting Firms Based on Their Degree of Internationalisation," *Journal of Business Research* 12(2), pp. 195-208.

Cavusgil, S.T. and V.H. Kirpalani (1993), "Introducing Products into Export Markets: Success Factors," *Journal of Business Research* 27(1), pp. 1-15.

Chaudhry, S. and D. Crick (1998), "Meeting the Needs of Different Ethnic Firms' Export Information Requirements: An Exploratory Study," *Business Information Review* 15(2), pp. 118-123.

Coviello, N.E. and H.J. Munro (1992), "Internationalizing the Entrepreneurial Technology-intensive Firm: Growth Through Linkage Development," in N. C. Churchill et al., eds., *Frontiers of Entrepreneurship Research*, Babson Park, Massachusetts: Center for Entrepreneurial Studies, pp. 430-443.

Coviello, N.E. and H.J. Munro (1995), "Growing the Entrepreneurial Firm: Networking for International Market Development," *European Journal of Marketing* 29(7), pp. 49-61.

Culpan, R. (1989), "Export Behavior of Firms: Relevance of Firm Size," *Journal of Business Research* 18(3), pp. 207-218.

Czinkota, M.R. (1994), "A National Export Assistance Policy for New and Growing Businesses," *Journal of International Marketing* 2, pp. 91-101.

Dana, L.P., H. Etemad and R.W. Wright (1998), "The Foundations and Evolution of International Entrepreneurship," Keynote Address at the International Conference on Globalisation and Emerging Businesses: Strategies for the 21st Century, Montreal, Canada, Sept. 26-28, 1998. Revised (1999), "Theoretical Foundations of International Entrepreneurship," in Richard W. Wright, ed., *International Entrepreneurship: Globalization of Emerging Businesses*, JAI Press, pp. 3-22.

Daniels, J.D. and L.H. Radebaugh (1995), *International Business* (7th Ed.), Reading, Massachusetts: Addison-Wesley Publishing Company.

Dichtl, E., M. Leibold, H.-G. Koglmayr and S. Mueller (1984), "The Export-Decision of Small and Medium-Sized Firms: A Review," *Management International Review* 24(2), pp. 49-60.

Donthu, N. and S.H. Kim (1993), "Implications of Firm Controllable Factors on Export Growth," *Journal of Global Marketing* 7(1), pp. 47-63.

D'Souza, D.E. and P.P. McDougall (1989), "Third World Joint Venturing: A Strategic Option for the Small Firm," *Entrepreneurship: Theory and Practice* 13(4), pp. 19-33.

Earley, P.C. and H. Singh (1995), "International and Intercultural Management Research," *Academy of Management Journal* 38(2), pp. 327-340.

Erramilli, M.K. and D.E. D'Souza (1993), "Venturing into Foreign Markets: The Case of the Small Service Firm," *Entrepreneurship: Theory and Practice* 17, pp. 29-41.

Ghauri, P.N. and S.M. Herbern (1994), "Export Behaviour of Smaller Norwegian Firms: Measuring the Effects of State Subsidies," *Journal of Euromarketing* 3(2), pp. 91-110.

Giamartino, G.A., P.P. McDougall and B.J. Bird (1993), "International Entrepreneurship: The State of the Field," *Entrepreneurship: Theory and Practice* 18(1), pp. 37-42.

Hansen, E.L. and T.H. Witkowski (1995), "Entrepreneur Involvement in International Marketing: The Effects of Overseas Social Networks and Self-Imposed Barriers to Action," in G. E. Hill et al., eds., *Research at the Marketing/Entrepreneurship Interface*, Chicago, Illinois: The University of Illinois at Chicago, pp. 363-367.

Hansen, N., K. Gillespie and E. Gencturk (1994), "SMEs and Export Involvement:

Market Responsiveness, Technology and Alliances," *Journal of Global Marketing* 7(4), pp. 7-27.

Hara, G. and T. Kanai (1994), "Entrepreneurial Networks Across Oceans to Promote International Strategic Alliances for Small Businesses," *Journal of Business Venturing* 9, pp. 489-507.

Holzmuller, H.H. and H. Kasper (1991), "On a Theory of Export Performance: Personal and Organisational Determinants of Export Trade Activities Observed in Small and Medium-sized Firms," *Management International Review* 31, pp. 45-70.

Jaffe, E.D. and H. Pasternak (1994), "An Attitudinal Model to Determine the Export Intention of Non-exporting, Small Manufacturers," *International Marketing Review* 11, pp. 17-32.

Johanson, J. and L.G. Mattsson (1988), "Internationalisation in Industrial Systems– A Network Approach," in N. Hood, ed., *Strategies for Global Competition*, London, UK: Croom Helm.

Johanson, J. and J.-E. Vahlne (1977), "The Internationalisation Process of the Firm– A Model of Knowledge Development and Increasing Foreign Market Commitment," *Journal of International Business Studies* 8, pp. 23-32.

Johanson, J. and F. Wiedersheim-Paul (1975), "The Internationalisation of the Firm: Four Swedish Cases," *Journal of International Management Studies* 12(3), pp. 36-64.

Jones, R. and R. Kustin (1995), "Supplier Relations and Export Activity in a Small-firm Grouping," *International Journal of Management* 12(1), pp. 112-122.

Katsikaes, C.S. (1994), "Export Competitive Advantages: The Relevance of Firm Characteristics," *International Marketing Review* 11(3), pp. 33-53.

Katsikeas, C.S., S.L. Deng and L.H. Wortzel (1997), "Perceived Export Success Factors of Small and Medium-sized Canadian Firms," *Journal of International Marketing* 5(4), pp. 53-72.

Keng, K.A. and T.S. Jiuan (1989), "Differences Between Small and Medium Sized Exporting and Non-exporting Firms: Nature or Nurture," *International Marketing Review* 6(4), pp. 27-40.

Kogut, B. (1985), "Designing Global Strategies: Profiting from Operational Flexibility," *Sloan Management Review* 27, pp. 27-38.

Kohn, T.O. (1997), "Small Firms as International Players," *Small Business Economics* 9(1), pp. 45-51.

Korhonen, H., R. Luostarinen and L. Welch (1996), "Internationalisation of SMEs: Inward-Outward Patterns and Government Policy," *Management International Review* 36(4), pp. 315-329.

Levie, J. (1994), "Can Governments Nurture Young Growing Firms? Quantitative Evidence from a Three-nation Study," in N. C. Churchill et al., eds., *Frontiers of Entrepreneurship Research*, Babson Park, Massachusetts: Babson College, 198-211.

Madsen, T.K. (1989), "Successful Export Marketing Management: Some Empirical Evidence," *International Marketing Review* 6(4), pp. 41-57.

Madsen, T.K. and P. Servais (1997), "The Internationalisation of Born Globals: An Evolutionary Process?" *International Business Review* 6(6), pp. 651-583.

McDougall, P.P. (1989), "International versus Domestic Entrepreneurship: New Venture Strategic Behavior and Industry Structure," *Journal of Business Venturing* 4(6), pp. 387-400.

McDougall, P.P. and B.M. Oviatt (1997), "International Entrepreneurship Literature in the 1990s and Directions for Future Research," in D. L. Sexton, and R.W. Smilor, eds., *Entrepreneurship 2000*, Chicago, Illinois: Upstart Publishing Company, pp. 291-320.

McDougall, P.P., S. Shane and B.M. Oviatt (1994), "Explaining the Formation of International New Ventures: The Limits of Theories from International Business Research," *Journal of Business Venturing* 9(6), pp. 469-487.

McDowell, D. and I. Rowlands (1995), "Export Information: A Case Study of SMEs in Northern Ireland," *Business Information Review* 11(4), pp. 43-53.

Moini, A.H. (1995), "An Inquiry into Successful Exporting: An Empirical Investigation Using a Three Stage Model," *Journal of Small Business Management* 33(3), pp. 9-25.

Moini, A.H. (1998), "Small Firms Exporting: How Effective Are Government Export Assistance Programs?" *Journal of Small Business Management* 36(1), pp. 1-15.

Nakos, G., K.D. Brouthers and L.E. Brouthers (1998), "The Impact of Firm and Managerial Characteristics on Small and Medium-sized Greek Firms' Export Performance," *Journal of Global Marketing* 11(4), pp. 23-47.

Ogbuehi, A.O. and T.A. Longfellow (1994), "Perceptions of U.S. Manufacturing SMEs Concerning Exporting: A Comparison Based on Export Experience," *Journal of Small Business Management* 32(4), pp. 37-47.

Oviatt, B.M. and P.P. McDougall (1994), "Toward a Theory of International New Ventures," *Journal of International Business Studies* 25(1), pp. 45-64.

Oviatt, B.M. and P.P. McDougall (1995), "Global Start-ups: Entrepreneurs on a Worldwide Stage," *The Academy of Management Executive* 9(2), pp. 30-43.

Oviatt, B.M. and P.P. McDougall (1997), "Challenges for Internationalisation Process Theory: The Case of International New Ventures," *Management International Review* 37(2), pp. 85-99.

Oviatt, B.M., P.P. McDougall, M. Simon and R.C. Shrader (1993), "Heartware International Corporation: A Medical Equipment Company Born International–Part A," *Entrepreneurship: Theory and Practice* 18(2), pp. 111-128.

Porter, M.E. (1985), *Competitive Advantage*, New York, NY: Free Press.

Ramaseshan, B. and M.A. Patton (1994), "Factors Influencing International Channel Choice of Small Businesses," *International Marketing Review* 11(4), pp. 19-34.

Reuber, A.R. and E. Fischer (1997), "The Influence of the Management Team's International Experience on the Internationalization Behaviors of SMEs," *Journal of International Business Studies* 28(4), pp. 807-825.

Riahi-Belkaoui, A. (1998), "The Effects of the Degree of Internationalisation on Firm Performance," *International Business Review* 7, pp. 315-321.

Tannous, G.F and A.K. Sarkar (1993), "Banks and Small Business Export Finance: New Targets for Services and Marketing Strategies," *The International Journal of Bank Marketing* 11(2), pp. 10-17.

Terpstra, V. and C.-M.J. Yu (1992), "Export Trading Companies: An American Trade Failure?" *Journal of Global Marketing* 6(3), pp. 29-54.

Triandis, H. (1980), "Introduction," in H. Triandis, and W.W. Lambert, eds., *Handbook of Cross-cultural Psychology, Vol. 1, Perspectives*, Boston, Massachusetts: Allyn and Bacon, pp. 1-14.

Walters, P.G. and S. Samie (1990), "A Model for Assessing Performance in Small U.S. Exporting Firms," *Entrepreneurship: Theory and Practice* 14, pp. 33-50.

Weaver, K.M., D. Berkowitz and L. Davies (1998), "Increasing the Efficiency of National Export Promotion Programs: The Case of Norwegian Exporters," *Journal of Small Business Management* 36(4), pp. 1-11.

Welch, L.S. (1992), "The Use of Alliances by Small Firms in Achieving Internationalisation," *Scandinavian International Business Review* 1(2), pp. 21-37.

Wright, P.C. (1993), "The Personal and the Personnel Adjustments and Costs to Small Businesses Entering the International Market Place," *Journal of Small Business Management* 31(1), pp. 83-93.

Zafarullah, M., M. Ali and S. Young (1998), "The Internationalisation of the Small Firm in Developing Countries–Exploratory Research from Pakistan," *Journal of Global Marketing* 11(3), pp. 21-40.

The Impact of Networks on New Zealand Firms

Aaron Sadler
Sylvie Chetty

SUMMARY. This article focuses on the network relationships that are established in the pre-export stages of a firm's development. It contributes to the literature by showing how firms use network relationships to overcome barriers to exporting and also to identify export opportunities. A conceptual model and hypotheses were developed from the literature and tested. This research is based on a postal survey of a cross-section of New Zealand exporting firms. The results show that business relationships both influence a firm's foreign market selection, and provide access to foreign markets that were not formerly considered by the firm. They also show that the key network actors are customer's customers and customer's suppliers. *[Article copies available for a fee from The Haworth Document Delivery Service: 1-800-342-9678. E-mail address: <getinfo@haworthpressinc.com> Website: <http://www.HaworthPress.com>]*

KEYWORDS. Networking, relationships, internationalisation, networks, synergy

INTRODUCTION

Previous research into the internationalisation of a firm has largely ignored the effects of network relationships in the pre-export stage.

Aaron Sadler and Sylvie Chetty are affiliated with Victoria University of Wellington, New Zealand.

[Haworth co-indexing entry note]: "The Impact of Networks on New Zealand Firms." Sadler, Aaron, and Sylvie Chetty. Co-published simultaneously in *Journal of Euromarketing* (International Business Press, an imprint of The Haworth Press, Inc.) Vol. 9, No. 2, 2000, pp. 37-58; and: *Global Marketing Co-Operation and Networks* (ed: Leo Paul Dana) International Business Press, an imprint of The Haworth Press, Inc., 2000, pp. 37-58. Single or multiple copies of this article are available for a fee from The Haworth Document Delivery Service [1-800-342-9678, 9:00 a.m. - 5:00 p.m. (EST). E-mail address: getinfo@haworthpress inc.com].

37

Instead, most studies on internationalisation have investigated firms that were already exporting in the hope of explaining the export process. The focus of this study is therefore on the network relationships that are established in the pre-export stages of a firm's development. This research contributes to the literature by showing how firms use those relationships to overcome barriers to exporting and to identify export opportunities within the networks.

It is important to study this area of pre-export behaviour and networks as it provides valuable insights about how firms can use and benefit from a synergistic relationship with other firms. These insights lead to explanations about how small to medium size firms make their export debuts and overcome such barriers as limited size, insufficient knowledge and few resources. In promoting exports, Trade New Zealand is using this network concept to encourage firms to collaborate and take advantage of benefits that networks offer firms. Trade New Zealand expedites the formation of collaborative relationships through its joint action groups, hard business networks and industry clusters.

LITERATURE REVIEW

Incremental Internationalisation Models

Several attempts have been made to conceptualise the export development phenomenon (Katsikeas and Leonidou, 1996) using the incremental approach. However, none of the incremental models appears to fully explain the internationalisation process (Katsikeas and Piercy, 1993). The first of the models emerged in 1975, developed by Johanson and Wiedersheim-Paul. It suggested that firms internationalise by an established chain of events. From no regular export activities, the firms export via independent representatives and then through a sales representative or subsidiary. This stages model emphasises the role of information acquisition to the incremental progress of the firm to internationalisation. Information available to the firm plays an important role in the firm's decision to export, highlighting the need for firms to develop networks to help them through the pre-export stage.

The most important barriers to exporting are internal to the firm (Leonidou, 1995). For non-exporters, the most important internal barriers are lack of foreign contacts, high initial investment, lack of information about exporting and insufficient personnel (Barker and Kaynak 1992). Tesar and Tarleton (1982) found that firms in the pre-export stage focus on identifying foreign market opportunities and Leonidou (1995) concluded that the limited availability of foreign market information constituted a major impediment. Both findings point to information collection as an important factor yet obtaining information about a foreign market is often costly and time-consuming, and hence a barrier for firms with limited resources.

The most important push for exporting is internal so that export stimulation factors are operating long before the firm makes its export debut (Leonidou, 1995). Any difficulties in the pre-export stage can lead to a passive attitude towards exporting (Leonidou, 1995). It can also lead to failures when the firm starts exporting and thus lead to a complete withdrawal (Welch and Weidersheim-Paul, 1980).

Pre-Export Behaviour Model

Only one pre-export behaviour model has been developed so far, by Olson and Wiedersheim-Paul (1978) who looked at the pre-export stage. They attempt to explain the process by which a firm moves from non-exporting to receiving its first export order.

The Olson and Wiedersheim-Paul (1978) model concentrates on the decision-maker's characteristics, the stimuli (external and internal influences) the decision-maker is exposed to, and the decision-maker's subsequent responses. All these influence the firm's pre-export behaviour.

Network Approach

The internationalisation literature using the network approach has essentially looked at firms that are already established exporters; it does not explain how networks are used in the pre-export stage of a firm's development. Axelsson and Easton (1992) define a network as "sets of two or more connected exchange relationships." Each member of the network does not necessarily have the same relationships as all the other members. The network itself evolves as firms interact with other firms, hence, is an evolving rather than a static entity (Hakansson, 1982).

Network activity is an important part of the continuing process of internationalisation (Welch and Welch, 1996), so it is helpful to study relationships in the pre-export stage. These relationships are developed over a period of time as the various parties interact (Forsgren and Johanson, 1992). Through interaction firms learn about each other's needs, capabilities and ways of doing business. Firms develop trust and invest resources into the relationship (Forsgren and Johanson, 1992). The boundaries between suppliers and customers become blurred. Competitors in the domestic market co-operate in foreign markets, becoming suppliers and customers to each other (Forsgren and Johanson, 1992).

While the Olson and Wiedersheim-Paul (1978) model has focused on the stimuli the firm is exposed to, the network approach focuses on the importance of relationships and networks to initiate export. The network approach looks at the role of exchange and how firms co-ordinate the activities and resources controlled by one actor with the activities and resources of another actor. This allows access to other resources controlled by other actors and makes it possible to co-ordinate activities of several actors. Firms are linked through technical bonds (common technology), personal/social bonds, and cognitive bonds (Johanson and Hallen, 1989). Hence, companies have knowledge of each other's resources, organisation, strategies and relationships.

Instead of focusing on the internal and external stimuli that face the firm in making the decision to internationalise, the network perspective suggests that the nature of relationships will influence strategic decisions. This extends the incremental approach to internationalisation, viewing the firm's strategy as an emerging pattern of behaviour influenced by a variety of network relationships (Welch and Welch, 1996). Both the internationalisation stages model and the network approach stress the cumulative nature of the firm's activities. The former focuses on the internal development of the firm's knowledge and other resources. The latter, however, offers a model of the market and the firm's relationship within the market (Johanson and Mattsson, 1988). It demonstrates how firms with a shortage of resources can use other actors in the network to access the resources that are available to them, such as distribution channels and offshore production facilities.

CENTRAL RESEARCH HYPOTHESES

Business Relationships:
Effects on Internationalisation Decisions

Internationalisation decisions such as the mode of market entry and which markets to enter are the most important when a firm considers exporting (Driscoll, 1995). Previous literature has sought to explain this incrementally, proposing that a firm's progress into the export arena was established through a series of stages (Johanson and Vahlne, 1977; Welch and Welch, 1996). These models do not consider the influence of other parties on export decisions, e.g., business relationships, influencing foreign market entry and choice of markets.

In their study of networks and internationalisation Coviello and Munro (1995) suggest that larger partners in a network affected international marketing conduct of smaller ones. Bell (1995) finds results in a similar vein that interfirm relationships appear influential in both selection and mode of foreign market entry for small firms. Hence, it is hypothesised that:

H1: Business relationships influence an exporting firm's foreign market selection. Additionally: These business relationships influence entry into markets not formerly considered by the firm.

H2: Business relationships influence the firm's entry mode into foreign markets.

Business Strategy:
Business Relationship Planning

Gomes-Casseres (1994) points to the growth of networks and alliances through the influence of the fast-moving global economy; it has led to firms establishing relationships with peers abroad so that companies can forge relationships in order to command competitive advantages they cannot achieve alone. Hence, they can use business relationships to fulfil the firm's strategic objectives, which may include building relationships to help expedite the internationalisation process of the firm. Welch and Welch (1996) discuss strategic networks in building links between a number of actors and find that they can develop results in both intended and unintended relationships. Thus, a firm's strategy in forming business relationships may result in unexpected market entry opportunities. It is hypothesised that:

H3: The strategic orientation of firms is to form business relationships in order to export.

H4: Business relationships are formed by a firm for the purpose of facilitating export.

Business Relationships: Effects in Overcoming Barriers to Export

Non-exporting firms see factors such as small firm size, limited financial resources, and limited market knowledge as inhibiting their internationalisation. Hence, through the establishment of business relationships firms can take advantage of the synergy created to help remove these barriers. This, during the initial export stages, is essential for the future success in international business endeavours (Leonidou, 1994). Hence, it is posited that:

H5: Exporting firms place high importance on forming business relationships to overcome export barriers. Specifically, exporters form business relationships to (a) overcome a lack of resources, (b) overcome a lack of foreign market knowledge and (c) overcome problems associated with a small firm size.

Business Relationships: Effect on Entry to Psychically Distant Markets

Literature based on the internationalisation process of the firm has largely described the patterns of internationalisation in two ways. The first, the incremental process, has already been referred to, although Hedlund and Kverneland (1984) found evidence that the internationalisation patterns of Swedish firms in Japan were not in accordance with those described by the model. The second description of internationalisation explains export to foreign markets of successively greater psychic distance (Johanson and Vahlne, 1990). Firms start by exporting to countries that are similar in terms of psychic distance (i.e., similar in terms of culture, language and political systems), then, as experience grows, to markets further away in terms of psychic distance. Hence, it is hypothesised that:

H6: Business relationships have an influence on a firm's market entry to psychically distant foreign markets.

The above is illustrated in Figure 1.

METHOD OF RESEARCH

Sample and Data Collection

This research is based on a postal survey of a cross-section of New Zealand exporting firms. The sample for this research was randomly selected from the *New Zealand Business Who's Who* (39th edition, 1998). This directory supplied a company name, address, contact person and the industry and products that the firm produced. Importantly, the list indicated whether the firm was an exporter. The responses received indicated that the database was flawed, as a number of firms that were non-exporters had inadvertently been included in the list as being exporters.

A pilot study was conducted with five Wellington-based exporting firms who were randomly selected from the *New Zealand Business Who's Who*. The interviewer was present when each respondent completed the questionnaire, to identify any potential problems with the questionnaire.

The sample size was 300 New Zealand exporting firms. A letter describing the study, a copy of the questionnaire, and a postage-paid return envelope were mailed to the manager or marketing executive of each of these New Zealand exporting firms. As an incentive respondents were offered a summary of the finished research results.

The covering letter also gave the authors' contact details for queries; the deadline for completed questionnaires, and a request that any non-exporting firm inadvertently contacted return the uncompleted questionnaire. In practice, respondents in this category simply wrote on the questionnaire or covering letter that they were not currently conducting export activities.

Completed questionnaires were numerically coded to ensure that respondents were removed from the database for the follow-up mail

FIGURE 1. Conceptual Model

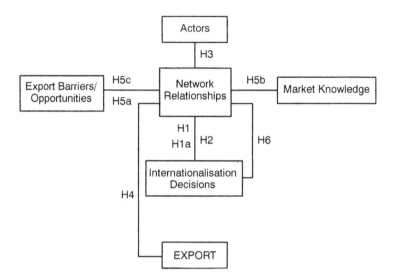

out. The follow-up took place two weeks after the deadline. The accompanying letter was almost identical to the earlier one with the addition of a paragraph highlighting the importance of the research. Another copy of the questionnaire was enclosed (in case the first had been misplaced) and a postage-paid addressed envelope for returning the questionnaire.

Of the 300 questionnaires in the first mail out, 148 were returned–a gross response rate of 49%. The first mail out generated 60 useable returns (gross 129 of which 44 were uncompleted and 25 returned by firms no longer exporting). The follow-up generated 6 more useable returns (gross 19, of which 10 were uncompleted and 3 returned by firms no longer exporting). The total gross response was 49%, with a total net response of 24%.

Testing for Validity and Reliability

As summarized in Table 1, this study used six multi-item scales to capture the various aspects of business relationships. These scales seek to measure the respondent's perception of barriers to export, the importance of obtaining knowledge from network actors, and the importance of resources via network actors, in the internationalisation

TABLE 1. Scale Reliability

Scale	Number of items	Standardised Alpha
Barriers to Export	(4 items)	0.7665
Knowledge	(5 items)	0.7546
Resources	(5 items)	0.8627
Foreign Access	(5 items)	0.8374
Foreign Entry	(5 items)	**0.6712**
Firm Size	(2 items)	0.8033
Export Debut	(7 items)	0.7549

process. The internal consistency of all but one scale exceeded 0.7, an acceptable threshold to confirm the reliability of the research scales (Cadogan and Diamantopoulos, 1996). The "foreign access" scale narrowly fell outside this threshold. However, it is assumed that this slight difference will have little effect on the final analysis and therefore that the measures used are reliable.

CONCEPTUALISATION OF CONSTRUCTS

The following definitions are included to clarify the meanings of the terms that are used to describe the constructs.

Actors

The actors construct refers to the external contributors of information to the firm. Primarily these include the firms' competitors, suppliers and customers. However, it is noted that there are third parties from which a firm may obtain information, such as a customer's customer. The actors construct is the important counterparts in the internationalisation process and can provide foreign market knowledge, or resources, which the firm utilises to internationalise.

The specific questions from within the questionnaire that relate to actors asks respondents to identify the parties with whom their firm has formed business relationships and the importance of those relationships, for example, in facilitating export.

Market Knowledge

The construct "market knowledge" refers to three different indicators of knowledge that firms may use as the basis for creating a network relationship. The first is experiential knowledge accumulated by the firm through experience with international operations. The second is local knowledge about such characteristics as the business climate, cultural patterns and structure of the market system (Johanson and Vahlne, 1977). The third aspect is technical knowledge about the firm's product or service; it could be in the form of a product innovation or technical "know how."

These three indicators capture the firm's use of knowledge or other network members to overcome any deficiencies of the firm in each of these areas. The quality of market knowledge may indicate the need to attract other network partners because of their technical knowledge or expertise. It may also highlight the importance of obtaining knowledge as part of the internationalisation process. Hence, the measurable variables of this construct relate to the three indicators already mentioned: experiential, technical and market knowledge. The extent to which a firm lacks any of these will encourage the formation of a business relationship with other actors.

Export Barriers/Opportunities

The export barriers/opportunities construct refers to the firm's size (number of full time employees and sales turnover) and to resources that encourage firms to initiate network relationships. A firm initiates a relationship because of a barrier or an opportunity; for example, using combined size to make a foreign market entry. Other resources provided could include the use of production facilities offshore, and access to distribution systems and personnel within the export country. Respondents were asked questions regarding the role which limited resources and the firm's size played in establishing business relationships.

Network Relationships

The network relationship construct refers to the various actors and the connected relationship partners within the network, of actors that the central firm has formed over time. It is the combination of the relationships that the firm has with other network "actors" as well as the market knowledge and firm size and resource factors. Hence, the business relationships with the various actors represent the entire network influences on the firm at any one point in time.

Essentially these relationships are established to overcome barriers to export or to take advantage of an opportunity from another network partner. There is an element of exchange where other network members obtain information from the firm. To determine the effects and the importance of this construct the respondents in the questionnaire were asked to describe the form of the relationships (formalised, informal) and the importance of maintaining and forming new business relationships.

Internationalisation Decisions

The internationalisation decisions construct refers to the crucial choices the firm is faced with once business relationships are established. It refers to the firm's choice of market entry and the means by which the new market is entered, such as by a joint venture, alliance or through an agent. It helps to describe how network relationships are used by firms to move into foreign markets, markets that are psychically distant from their own. O'Grady and Lane (1996) describe psychic distance as the differences in culture, language, industry structure and competitive environment between countries.

The construct also indicates how network partners influence a firm's decision and how relationships propel a firm into certain export markets. The questionnaire asks about the effects of business relationships on market entry and the means of entry, e.g., joint venture, and the extent to which the foreign market selection was made by the firm or by the business relationship "actor."

Export

This construct refers to the firm's fulfilment of a foreign export order. Once the process of selecting a foreign market and the means of entry are decided, this construct completes the export process. The firm has internationalised and become an exporter. Alternatively the export construct can represent firms that have ceased to export but then re-establish export through business relationships. Whereas the market entry and mode construct attempts to identify the form of export and the means of foreign market selection through business relationships, the export construct attempts to measure the "how" facet, particularly how the export order was filled after the market was selected.

RESEARCH FINDINGS

Analysis and Results

This section provides background information about the firms surveyed and outlines the statistical analysis and results of the hypotheses tested. The software statistics package SPSS (Statistics Package for the Social Sciences, Version 7) was used to generate the results for the various tests conducted. Eighty-three percent of respondents indicated that export was part of their firm's planned strategy. Table 2 shows the frequency of choice of foreign markets.

Two forms of statistical tests were used to analyse the data collected from the questionnaires: bivariate non-parametric correlation and the Kruskal-Wallis comparison of independent means test. The Kruskal-Wallis test was used to analyse the data for Hypothesis 4; all other analyses used simple correlations between variables. The Kruskal-Wallis test is a non-parametric version of a one-way ANOVA (Analysis of Variance) test. This test determines whether two or more groups have the same median.

The Spearman's rho correlation was used to test relationships between two variables (this was preferred to the Pearson's correlation coefficient due to the ordinal nature of the data); the correlation coefficient provides an indication of the strength of the relationship thus providing evidence that one variable is positively (or negatively) related to another. However, correlation does not imply evidence of cause and effect (Cooper and Emory, 1995). Hence, this is an impor-

TABLE 2. Choice of Foreign Markets

		Frequency	Percent
Major export markets	Australia	24	36.4
	UK/Europe	13	19.7
	North America	10	15.1
	Asia	19	28.8
	Total	**66**	**100**
First foreign market entered by firm	Australia	34	51.5
	UK/Europe	8	12.1
	Africa/Middle East	1	1.5
	North America	8	12.2
	Asia	15	22.7
	Total	**66**	**100**

tant consideration when interpreting the results, suggesting that any significant statistical findings provide only an indication that X may cause Y; other variables may have an influence on these variables.

Business Relationships

H1: Business relationships influence an exporting firms' foreign market selection. Additionally: These business relationships influence entry into markets not formerly considered by the firm.

H2: Business relationships influence the firms' entry mode into foreign markets.

Two items were correlated against a single variable to test the first hypothesis; this single variable (foreign decision) measures the importance of business relationships in deciding which foreign markets to enter. The other two items (foreign access and foreign entry) measure the importance of business relationships in providing access to, and entry in, foreign markets. Each of these two items is made up of the various network actors which respondents score in terms of the level of importance for each relationship.

The initial correlation results, using a summated scale of all the relationships, indicate a significant relationship between a firm's business relationships and the foreign market selected for export (Spearman's rho = 0.346; Sig = 0.002). Further correlations comparing the "foreign decision" variable to the individual "actors" revealed the key single relationships which have the most impact on a firm's foreign market entry, and the foreign markets which they are provided access via these relationships. The tabulated results below (Table 3) indicate three significant relationships that affect a firm's entry in foreign markets, namely customers, customers' customers and suppliers.

Additionally, the "foreign decision" variable was correlated with "foreign access," which measures the importance of business relationships in providing access to other foreign markets. This relationship was tested in the same manner as above, with the results revealing strikingly similar results. The correlation between the summated scale of the entire network actors and the item "foreign access" indicated a significant result (Spearman's rho = 0.370; Sig = 0.001). The individual results identified the same three network actors as being important in providing access to other foreign markets (Table 4).

TABLE 3. Foreign Decision and Foreign Entry (All Relationships)

	Actor	Spearman's rho	Significance
Foreign Decision	Customer**	0.482	0.000
	Customers' customer**	0.348	0.002
	Suppliers*	0.231	0.032
	Suppliers' suppliers	0.048	0.351
	Competitors	0.123	0.165

** Correlation is significant at the 0.01 level (1 tailed).
* Correlation is significant at the 0.05 level (1 tailed).

TABLE 4. Foreign Decision and Foreign Access

	Actor	Spearman's rho	Significance
Foreign Decision	Customer**	0.469	0.000
	Customers' customer**	0.405	0.000
	Suppliers**	0.334	0.003
	Suppliers' suppliers	0.143	0.126
	Competitors	0.113	0.182

** Correlation is significant at the 0.01 level (1 tailed).

The correlation results for H1a indicate a highly significant relationship between the items "foreign decision" and "markets not formerly considered" (Spearman's coefficient = 0.644; Sig = 0.000). This suggests that business relationships are highly influential in a firm's decision to enter markets not formerly considered as export destinations. Therefore business relationships are important in providing access to foreign markets which the firm may not have considered for a number of different reasons, such as accessibility to distribution networks. It could be quite possible that these firms simply did not consider these markets because of the strategic focus of the firm prior to the opportunities presented by these business relationships.

The analysis of Hypothesis 2 sought to measure the influence of business relationships on the mode of entry used by the firm. This hypothesis assumes that firms that indicate that business relationships were highly important in deciding to export will thus be influenced to use a particular mode of entry for their initial export. However, it is noted that it is highly possible that this is not so, and that those firms may have entered a foreign market without any influence from other network actors, thus the mode of entry utilised was not influenced by any business relationship.

The results imply a positive relationship between these two variables (Spearman's rho = 0.240; Sig = 0.032). This suggests that the mode of entry used by the firm to fulfil its first export order may be influenced by other business relationships. For example, a joint venture may be the first method used to fulfil the firm's initial export order because an opportunity has arisen from within the business network or perhaps because of advice from other business relationships.

Business Strategy

H3: The strategic orientation of firms is to form business relationships in order to export.

H4: Business relationships are formed by a firm for the purpose of facilitating export.

As illustrated in Table 5, the analysis of Hypothesis 3 reveals that firms place some importance on establishing business relationships in order to enter the export field (Spearman's rho = 0.289; Sig = 0.009). The firms perhaps understand the importance of business relationships in aiding their strategic plan to internationalise, i.e., to export, and this is their chief driving motive.

The purpose of forming these relationships may be for the purpose of fulfiling other objectives such as obtaining foreign market knowledge. The correlation result from the analysis of Hypothesis 4 yielded a negative correlation coefficient (Spearman's rho = −0.448; Sig = 0.000) suggesting an inverse relationship between the two variables. An inverse relationship suggests that large values of the first variable are associated with small values of the second variable, and vice versa (Cooper and Emory, 1995). Therefore, in this instance firms that place high importance on forming business relationships (a high value) may place low importance (a low value) on forming relationships for the sole purpose of starting export activities. Thus no evidence was found to support the hypothesis that firms form business relationships for the sole purpose of internationalising. Instead business relationships may be formed for a myriad of other reasons, such as obtaining foreign market knowledge or collecting information regarding international activities (processes, legal requirements, etc.).

The Kruskal-Wallis test was then used to determine which individual relationships were the most significant in initiating export. The two items used in the test were "export strategy" and "export debut." The latter item (export debut) is comprised of a number of different network actors (Table 6). Hence, the results of this test will indicate which business relationships are influential in a firm's decision to begin exporting.

The results indicate that several relationships have an influence on a firm initiating export activities, notably those with competitors, supplier, suppliers' suppliers and formal co-operative agreements. No single relationship spawns a firm's decision to begin exporting.

TABLE 5. Business Relationship Planning

Hypothesis	Items Correlated	Spearman's rho	Sig.
H3	Importance of Seeking New Business Relationships Impact of Business Relationships	0.289	0.009
H4	Export Debut Export Strategy	− 0.448	0.000

TABLE 6. Export Strategy and Export Debut

	Actor	Chi-Square	Asymp. Sig.
Export Strategy	Customer	0.566	0.452
	Customers' customer	3.136	0.077
	Competitors	7.865	0.005
	Suppliers	7.067	0.008
	Suppliers' suppliers	12.142	0.000
	Government agencies	2.98	0.084
	Formal co-operative agreements	9.832	0.002

Effects in Overcoming Barriers to Export

H5: Exporting firms place high importance on forming business relationships to overcome export barriers. Specifically, exporters form business relationships to (a) overcome a lack of resources, (b) overcome a lack of foreign market knowledge, and (c) overcome problems associated with a small firm size.

The first statement posited in Hypothesis 5 suggests that, collectively, barriers to export provide an obstacle to a firm internationalising. Furthermore, business relationships are formed to overcome these barriers. However, upon analysis the collective measure of export barriers and the importance of forming business relationships appear to have no significant relationship (Spearman's rho = 0.202; Sig = 0.61). In addition the results of Hypothesis 5(a) and 5(c) also failed to produce any significant results (Spearman's rho = 0.45; Sig = 0.361 and Spearman's rho = 0.081; Sig = 0.262, respectively).

The results of Hypothesis 5(b) did provide evidence that business relationships are formed to overcome barriers relating to obtaining foreign market knowledge (Spearman's rho = 0.239; Sig = 0.027). Further correlations of the individual actors relating to obtaining market knowledge revealed that the firms' customers (Spearman's rho = 0.335; Sig = 0.003) and customers' customers (Spearman's rho = 0.256; Sig = 0.019) were the most important contributors in terms of providing market knowledge. Results are summarized in Table 7.

Effect on Entry to Psychically Distant Markets

H6: Business relationships have an influence on a firm's market entry to psychically distant foreign markets.

As indicated in Table 8, the analysis of the final research hypothesis reveals no significant relationship between the influence of business relationships and the entry to psychically distant markets (Spearman's rho = 0; Sig = 0.120).

This suggests that New Zealand firms perhaps follow more of an incremental approach to internationalisation, as described by Johanson and Vahlne (1977), where firms export to countries with increasing psychic distance as they gain experience and knowledge of foreign export operations and processes. Just over half of respondents indi-

TABLE 7. Effects on Overcoming Barriers to Export

Hypothesis	Items Correlated	Spearman's rho	Sig.
H5	Importance of Seeking New Business Relationships Barriers to Export	0.202	0.610
H5a	Importance of Seeking New Business Relationships Resources	0.45	0.361
H5b	Importance of Seeking New Business Relationships Knowledge	0.239	0.270
H5c	Importance of Seeking New Business Relationships Firm Size	0.081	0.262

TABLE 8. Importance of Seeking New Relationships

	Actor	Spearman's rho	Significance
Importance of	Customer**	0.335	0.003
Seeking New	Customers' customer*	0.256	0.019
Relationships	Suppliers	0.123	0.162
	Suppliers' suppliers	0.024	0.425
	Competitors	0.189	0.064

** Correlation is significant at the 0.01 level (1 tailed).
* Correlation is significant at the 0.05 level (1 tailed).

cated that the first foreign market entered was Australia (51.5%), which is the closest foreign market in terms of psychic distance to New Zealand. A further 12.1% of respondents indicated that Europe was their first foreign market entered, also a market relatively close in terms of psychic distance.

DISCUSSION

Our results provide evidence to suggest that business relationships have an influence on both a firm's decision to select certain foreign markets, and markets not formerly considered as export destinations. Two of the hypothesised results highlight the same network actors as having the largest impact on market selection and markets not formerly considered for export. These relationships are those between the firm and their customers, customers' customers and suppliers.

Welch and Welch (1996) suggest that it is difficult for companies to include networks in the strategic planning cycle. Because networks are intangible, their strategic value is minimised. However, the hypotheses relating to business relationships planning revealed that firms in this research understand the importance of those relationships in providing benefits and opportunities. The results indicate that these firms place high strategic importance on forming relationships to aid their internationalisation. However, these relationships are unlikely to be driven by the sole desire of the firm to start exporting. The results of Hypothesis 4 indicate a negative relationship between the variables "export strategy" and "export debut" (Spearman's rho = -0.448; Sig = 0.000). This can be interpreted as the firm having a strategic objective to export, and the building of these various relationships are seen as collectively building towards the firm making their international debut, rather than any one relationship driving the firm into export.

The research results suggest that, collectively, barriers to export appear to have little impact on a firm's decision to start exporting. However, breaking down this construct and testing the individual aspects of export barriers revealed some interesting results. For example, the results within this research suggest that the size of the firm (number of full time employees and sales turnover) does not present a significant barrier to New Zealand firms wishing to export. These findings may seem surprising considering the relative size of the firms sampled, 72.8% of firms had less than 50 full time employees, 54.5% of firms earned less than $10 million per annum, which would be considered small in comparison to other countries.

Previous literature provides some debate as to the significance of the firm's size in the internationalisation process. Coviello and Munro (1997) have already highlighted the technological intensiveness of the product offered and small production runs to niche markets as two possible explanations for size not being a barrier to small software firms in New Zealand. They found that in a relationship between a small firm and a multinational company (Wang), the small firm obtained market access through Wang's international subsidiaries; in return Wang gained the rights to the technological capabilities offered by the small firm. Thus, despite the software firm's small size (in terms of number of full-time employees and annual turnover), the technology developed by this firm overcame any obstacles associated with this factor.

CONCLUSION

Business relationships influence a firm's foreign market selection, and access to foreign markets that it had not formerly considered. Further, the key network actors were customers, customers' customers and suppliers. From these relationships the firm is able to learn about the internationalisation process. This learning is critical to the firm as it helps reduce uncertainty and risk perceptions of international operations (Welch and Welch, 1996). The managerial implication of this finding is that those firms seeking to export should be targeting these specific relationships if they wish to internationalise. Furthermore, this internal knowledge factor is critical to successful international operations.

This research suggests that any one relationship by itself is probably not sufficient to provide the entire knowledge needed for the firm to internationalise. Additionally, each relationship should be seen as building towards the strategic goal of initiating export activities. This collective information obtained from various network actors will better equip the firm for their international debut.

The findings within this research provide clear evidence that the building of business relationships offer distinct advantages, such as overcoming barriers to entry and enabling access to foreign markets. This has a clear policy implication for government in the development of export activities within New Zealand. Hence, any trade assistance scheme or other policy initiatives that seek to promote export should be educating firms on the benefits that collaboration offers within a network environment.

FUTURE RESEARCH DIRECTIONS AND LIMITATIONS

One limitation is that this study provides only a historical view of a firm's progress from domestic supplier to exporter. Whilst this illustrates the influence of business relationships, the specific details of how and why relationships were formed did not emerge. Therefore, suggested future research is a qualitative study of exporting firms to determine those details.

Another limitation of this study is that it excludes non-exporters. A longitudinal study of firms that progress from non-exporter to exporter would provide a useful direction for further investigation into the effects of business relationships in the internationalisation process. Time and financial constraints meant that this type of study could not be undertaken within this research.

REFERENCES

Axelsson, B. and G. Easton, eds. (1992), *Industrial Networks: A View of Reality*, London: Routledge.

Barker, A. and E. Kaynak (1992), "An Empirical Investigation of the Differences Between Initiating and Continuing Exporters," *European Journal of Marketing* 26 (3).

Bell, J. (1995), "The Internationalisation of Small Computer Software Firms–A Further Challenge to 'Stage' Theories," *European Journal of Marketing* 29 (8).

Cadogan, J. and A. Diamantopoulos (1996), "Measuring Market Orientation in an Export Context," Working Paper, University of Wales-Swansea.

Cooper, D. and C. Emory (1995), *Business Research Methods* (5th Edition), United States: Irwin.

Coviello, N. and H. Munro (1995), "Growing the Entrepreneurial Firm: Networking for International Market Development," *European Journal of Marketing* 29 (7), pp. 49-61.

Coviello, N. and H. Munro (1997), "Network Relationships and the Internationalisation Process of Small Software Firms," *International Business Review*, 6 (4) 1997, pp. 361-386.

Driscoll, A. (1995), "Foreign Market Entry Methods: A Mode Choice Framework," in S. Paliwoda J. Ryans, *International Marketing Reader*, London: Routledge, pp. 15-34.

Ford, D. (1990), *Understanding Business Markets: Interaction, Relationships and Networks*, London: Academic Press.

Forsgren, M. and J. Johanson (1992), *Managing Networks in International Business*, Amsterdam: Gordon and Breach.

Gomes-Casseres, B. (1994) "Group versus Group: How Alliance Networks Compete," *Harvard Business Review*, July/August, pp. 62-74.

Hakansson, H. (1982), *International Marketing and Purchasing of Industrial Goods*, Chichester: Wiley.

Hedlund, G. and A. Kverneland (1984), *Investing in Japan: The Experience of Swedish Firms*, Institute of International Business, Stockholm School of Economics.

Johanson, J. and L. Mattsson (1988), "Internationalisation in Industrial Systems: A

Network Approach," in P. J. Buckley, and P.N. Ghauri, eds., *The Internationalisation of the Firm: A Reader*, London: Academic Press, pp. 303-321.

Johanson, J. and L. Hallen (1989), "Networks of Relationships in International Industrial Marketing," *Advances in International Marketing* 3, pp. 195-197.

Johanson, J. and J. Vahlne (1977) "The Internationalisation Process of the Firm: A Model of Knowledge Development and Increasing Foreign Commitments," *Journal of International Business Studies* 8 (1), pp. 23-32.

Johanson, J. and J. Vahlne (1990), "The Mechanism of Internationalisation," *International Marketing Review* 7 (4), pp. 11-24.

Johanson, J. and F. Wiedersheim-Paul (1975), "The Internationalisation of the Firm: Four Swedish Cases," *Journal of Management Studies*, October, pp. 305-322.

Katsikeas, C. and L. Leonidou (1996), "The Export Development Process: An Integrative Review of Empirical Models," *Journal of International Business Studies* 27 (3).

Katsikeas, C. and N. Piercy (1993), "Long-term Export Stimuli and Firm Characteristics in a European LDC," *Journal of International Marketing* 1 (3), pp. 239-256.

Kedia, B. and J. Chhokar (1986), "Factors Inhibiting Export Performance of Firms: An Empirical Investigation," *Management International Review* 26(4), pp. 33-43.

Leonidou, L. (1994), "Export Barriers: Non-exporters' Perceptions," *International Marketing Review* 12 (1), September, pp. 4-25.

Leonidou, L. (1995), "Export Stimulation: A Non-exporter's Perspective," *European Journal of Marketing* 29 (8), pp. 17-36.

Lindqvist, M. (1988), "Internationalisation of Small Technology-Based Firms: Three Illustrative Case Studies on Swedish Firms," Stockholm School of Economics Research Paper 88/15.

Macdonald, S. (1992), "Information Networks and the Exchange of Information," in C. Antonelli, ed., *The Economics of Information Networks*, Amsterdam: Elsevier, pp. 51-69.

Mattsson, L. (1997), "Relationship Marketing and the Markets as Networks Approach: A Comparative Analysis of Two Evolving Streams of Research," *Journal of Marketing Management*.

O'Grady, S. and H. Lane (1996), "The Psychic Distance Paradox," *Journal of International Business Studies*, Second Quarter, pp. 309-333.

Olson, H. and F. Wiedersheim-Paul (1978), "Factors Affecting the Pre-Export Behavior of Non-Exporting Firms," in M. Ghertman and J. Leontiadas, eds., *European Research in International Business*, New York, pp. 283-305.

Tesar, G. and J.S. Tarleton (1982), "Comparison of Wisconsin and Virginian Small and Medium-sized Exporters: Aggressive and Passive Exporters," in M.R. Czinkota and G. Tesar, eds., *Export Management*, New York: Praeger.

Welch, D. and L. Welch (1996), "The Internationalisation Process and Networks: A Strategic Management Perspective," *Journal of International Marketing* 4 (3), pp. 11-28.

Welch, L. and F. Wiedersheim-Paul (1980), "Initial Exports–A Marketing Failure?" *Journal of Management Studies*, October, pp. 333-344.

An Export Grouping Scheme

Denice Welch
Lawrence Welch
Ian Wilkinson
Louise Young

SUMMARY. In this essay, research on a new demand-driven export grouping scheme initiated by the trade promotion authority in Australia is reported. The research involved a qualitative, evaluative study of the first two so-called joint action groups formed under the scheme. The basis of formation of the groups was that a clear foreign market opportunity existed. As part of the evaluation, particular emphasis was given to the impact that a strong market goal had on group formation and operation. It was found that the group goal effect, stressed as important in organisational behaviour literature, played an important, positive role in the functioning of the group. However, group dynamics issues also appeared to have a significant effect on outcomes: specifically, group size, composition, and cohesion; along with an important facilitation role performed by the project manager for each group who was appointed by the trade promotion authority. In both groups, the difficult task was to build group cohesion at the same time as undertaking action to achieve the foreign market goal. *[Article copies available for a fee from The Haworth Document Delivery Service: 1-800-342-9678. E-mail address: <getinfo@haworthpressinc.com> Website: <http://www.HaworthPress.com>]*

KEYWORDS. Internationalisation, exporting, group dynamics, Australia

Denice Welch and Lawrence Welch are affiliated with the Norwegian School of Management, Oslo, Norway. Ian Wilkinson is affiliated with the University of Western Sydney-Nepean, Australia. Louise Young is affiliated with the University of Technology, Sydney, Australia.

[Haworth co-indexing entry note]: "An Export Grouping Scheme." Welch, Denice et al. Co-published simultaneously in *Journal of Euromarketing* (International Business Press, an imprint of The Haworth Press, Inc.) Vol. 9, No. 2, 2000, pp. 59-84; and: *Global Marketing Co-Operation and Networks* (ed: Leo Paul Dana) International Business Press, an imprint of The Haworth Press, Inc., 2000, pp. 59-84. Single or multiple copies of this article are available for a fee from The Haworth Document Delivery Service [1-800-342-9678, 9:00 a.m. - 5:00 p.m. (EST). E-mail address: getinfo@haworthpressinc.com].

INTRODUCTION

As research on internationalisation has developed, there has been an inevitable concern with its implications for export promotion schemes. This has led to many suggestions about how to effectively encourage improved export performance both in terms of getting exporters started and sustaining foreign market expansion (Cavusgil and Czinkota, 1990; Seringhaus and Rosson, 1990). At the same time, governments have been under political and economic pressure to stimulate increased international business activity by domestic companies. A wide variety of new initiatives in export promotion in various countries have resulted from this concern, as governments continue to search for better ways in which to play a positive facilitation role (Luostarinen, Korhonen, Jokinen, and Pelkonen, 1994; Department of Foreign Affairs and Trade, 1995). One reason for this continued quest is that past approaches have been regarded as being of limited success (Kedia and Chhokar, 1986; Nothdurft, 1992). It has led to a re-examination of old techniques, such as export grouping schemes, in the light of new thinking about strategic alliances and networks (Ferris, 1985; Strandell, 1985; Welch and Joynt, 1987). For example, a new scheme, involving the establishment of "export circles" in Finland, has the requirement that each circle be kept small and that the companies concerned should be non-competitive (Luostarinen et al., 1994).

In general, an export grouping scheme provides the opportunity for member companies to spread the initial costs and risks of international market entry, share information and experiences, and pool resources to support stronger promotional efforts. Small firms particularly have been viewed as a segment which could benefit from the extra resources and marketing impact obtained by acting in combination with other companies (Welch, 1992). The potential of a group, though, is often negated by the difficulties experienced in persuading various individuals to work together for the common good.

For export grouping schemes to succeed, member companies are required to accept group-determined goals and activities, which is particularly difficult for independent owners of small companies, and even more so when the group comprises competitors (Welch and Joynt, 1987). As Van de Ven has noted: "Organisations do not co-ordinate for co-ordination's sake. Instead, organisations strain to maintain their autonomy" (1976, p. 28). Member companies must be convinced that the rewards of joining the group will outweigh the costs–what Forsyth (1990, p. 63) describes as the "minimax" principle associated with social exchange theory: "People will join groups that provide them with the maximum number of valued rewards while incurring the fewest number of possible costs." Should the costs of remaining in a group be perceived as being higher than the benefits, members may withdraw from the group. It would also appear that group dynamics (the social processes and interactions within groups) play an important role in determining the outcome of export grouping schemes. For example, in early research into export marketing groups by the Organization for Economic Co-operation and Development (OECD), it was found that one of the main causes of failure was "unwillingness to cooperate" (1964, p. 11). However, limited research has been undertaken in the export marketing field on the impact of grouping issues and their effect on the operation and performance of export grouping schemes (Cavusgil and Czinkota, 1990; Seringhaus and Rosson, 1990).

In this paper, we analyse and assess a new exporting initiative undertaken in Australia, called the Joint Action Group (JAG) Scheme, with particular emphasis on the impact of grouping issues on outcomes. The JAG Scheme was initiated by officials within Austrade (the Australian Trade Commission), a semi-government instrumentality. Austrade is effectively the trade promotion arm of the Australian government. The scheme represented an attempt to use the grouping format as a way of improving the performance of Australian exporters.

RESEARCH METHOD

The research, conducted by the authors, was part of an evaluation study of the JAG Scheme, commissioned by Austrade. At the time of study, only two JAGs had been in operation for what was considered a sufficient period to enable group processes and outcomes to be investigated.

Given the research emphasis on process, and a need to examine the operations of the JAGs in-depth, a qualitative case study approach was deemed appropriate (Patton, 1990; Stake, 1994; Yin, 1994). In this context, the case was the JAG Scheme, with the phenomenon under investigation the formation and operation of each JAG (the unit of analysis). The evaluation was carried out over a period of about six months. Further information on the progress of each JAG was provided by an Austrade contact person subsequent to the formal reporting of the results of the evaluation. Data were collected through semi-structured interviews with:

- Six Austrade officials connected with the scheme, including the two Project Managers for each JAG;
- Hay JAG: nine oaten hay processors (six current members, one withdrawn, two non-members); and three members of the legal firm;
- China Grain JAG: seven JAG Board members, five current members, three withdrawn, and two non-members.

All interviews were tape-recorded. Two teams, each comprising two researchers (the authors), conducted the interviews. Content validity was enhanced through this use of investigator triangulation, providing a check on bias in data collection and analysis (Patton, 1990). The researchers were granted full access to all documentation held on file within Austrade, thus enabling data triangulation. Data verification was also obtained through the use of the Project Managers' factual confirmation of the final case report. Interview transcripts were subsequently content analysed by both research teams. Emergent themes and patterns relating to grouping issues were labelled using analyst-constructed typologies which were derived from both international marketing and group dynamics literature (Patton, 1990).

AUSTRADE'S JAG SCHEME

Most export grouping schemes have tended to take a "supply-based" approach to the formation and operation of the export group (Nothdurft, 1992), as illustrated in Figure 1. This has meant that an important part of the initial activity focused on finding appropriate firms (however defined), coaxing them to join the group, and then formally establishing the group. Although international market penetration (perhaps with a focus on one particular foreign market or region) is the argument for the group's formation, nevertheless the international marketing activity often tends to be consequent upon

FIGURE 1. Export Grouping Schemes

General Aim: Improve international market

"Supply"-based

Form group
↓
Decide on activities, markets,
membership, fees, etc.
↓
Foreign market research
(opportunity(ies) exposed?)

"Demand"-based

Specific foreign market
opportunity(ies) exposed
(e.g., through Austrade post)
↓
Form group (JAG) to
exploit opportunity(ies)

FOREIGN MARKET ACTIVITY
Penetration through acting jointly

group establishment (Welch and Joynt, 1987). Indeed, based on Swedish research, Stenberg argues that "the conditions for a successful performance come from within. Only when a group has managed to create technical and social agreement can the market begin to be penetrated" (1982, p. 181).

However, given the normal difficulties of group establishment and maintenance, there is a tendency for the vehicle (the group) to almost become the end rather than the means, and for its continuance to be judged in itself as a criterion of success. This may reflect the position of some advocates who have a vested interest (such as consulting fees) in the continuity of the group, and as an argument for forming further groups.

The Australian Joint Action Group (JAG) Scheme could be termed a "demand driven" approach to export grouping (Figure 1). The initial focus, indeed the very basis for existence of the group, is a specific, concrete, international market prospect. The idea is to create the group as a means of capturing the market opportunity. In this sense, it is the market that drives the grouping process and subsequent activities. In line with goal-setting theory (O'Leary-Kelly, Martocchio and Frink, 1994), this gives the scheme the advantage of a tangible goal that provides a reason for companies to join the group. As well, there was an underlying belief by the scheme's initiators that members of a JAG would be more likely to remain involved and committed to both the group and the international activity because such a demand-driven approach would provide well-defined objectives.

Typical of such agencies, Austrade maintains a global network of trade offices, which gather and disseminate relevant foreign market information as well as performing a promotional role for Australian firms within these foreign markets. It was envisaged that Austrade would maintain an active role in a JAG for a period of around two years, by which time it was considered that a JAG should be relatively self-sufficient.

Once the JAG Scheme was established, Austrade's foreign offices became the front line in identifying concrete market prospects that were deemed amenable to exploitation via a group of Australian exporters. Each opportunity was to be signalled to the relevant section within Austrade's Australian headquarters, where its potential for forming a JAG was assessed. With the publicity generated by the operation of the first JAGs, various industry representatives, having identified foreign market opportunities, have since approached Austrade directly for support in forming JAGs. As illustrated in Figure 2, the signals for JAG possibilities eventually came to Austrade from both its foreign offices and within Australian industry. In the latter case, industry representatives had to convince Austrade of the viability of the market opportunity and industry capability (in both marketing and grouping terms).

FORMATION OF THE FIRST JAGS

The first moves to establish JAGs began in 1992, in response to two clearly identified opportunities for group action: the World Bank's China Grain Distribution and Marketing project; and oaten hay exports to Japan. The China Grain project, co-funded by the World Bank and the Chinese government, aimed at improving the efficiency of China's grain handling and distribution system; in essence moving from bag to bulk storage and handling. Australian industry was a late contender for the design and construction work associated with this project. It was felt within Austrade that such a large (over $1 billion US) and multi-faceted project would demand a more co-ordinated

FIGURE 2. JAG–A Response to an Opportunity

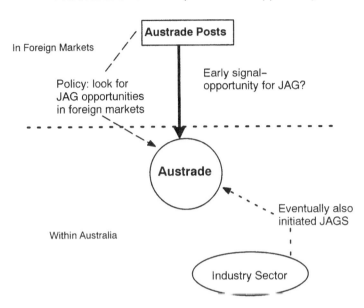

approach by Australian industry–partly because of a preference for this on the Chinese side, but also because other competitor countries (such as Canada) were using a government-supported, combined marketing strategy.

Once alerted to the project, Austrade played an instrumental role in generating interest within Australian industry. It called three public meetings, in late 1992, as a means of informing relevant companies of the project's potential and suggesting the JAG vehicle as a way of positioning Australian efforts for the design and construction stages. During the first year, 34 organisations joined to form the JAG, comprising both complementary and competitive firms, and covering a wide range across the industry spectrum: large consulting, design and construction firms; semi-government organisations such as the Australian wheat marketing authority (Australian Wheat Board) and grain handling authorities; and various-sized firms involved in providing software and equipment for grain storage and handling. The JAG operated through a company structure: Australia Grain Technology Export Promotion Limited (AGTEP).

The Oaten Hay JAG was formed to develop a more co-ordinated

and market-responsive approach to the Japanese market. With the increase in demand for beef and dairy products, Japan has become an important market for livestock feed. Australian oaten hay processors began exporting to Japan in the early 1980s in response to this demand. Each processor contracted with a large number of growers for the supply of hay, which was processed into packs and shipped to Japan. The processors were dispersed through the major hay growing areas of southern Australia. While these exporters had achieved some penetration of the Japanese market, by the end of the 1980s, this had stabilised at a relatively low level (about 5% of the total market), and there were problems associated with the quality and reliability of the supply.

Unlike the China Grain approach of public forums, Austrade identified and invited major oaten hay processors (except one processor who was perceived as being a likely disruptive element) to a meeting in late 1992 at which the JAG concept was discussed. Initially, ten processors agreed to the formation of a JAG, representing about 75% of Australian oaten hay exports to Japan. They contributed financially to enable the JAG to operate through a company structure: Australian Hay Pty. Ltd., even though they were effectively competitors in the Japanese market.

OPERATION AND OUTCOMES

In both JAGs, membership fees provided financial resources to assist in group promotional activities, and they were also able to access additional financial support through government agencies. The financial base contributed to the employment of a dedicated Project Manager from Austrade for each JAG.

Hay JAG

Interview data show that, for the Hay members, the formal JAG meetings provided an important forum for interaction, particularly as the processors came from different states of Australia, and some had not met previously. While these formal meetings occurred infrequently, informal contact between members increased over time, with information-sharing on issues of common interest. This facilitated the operation of the JAG, enabling co-ordination of approaches to group problems such as transport, packaging, pricing, and response to the 1994-1995 drought in the Eastern States. Visits to each others' plants and technology-related discussions were also cited as examples of cooperation. The informal contact and relationship-building came to be seen by members as a positive outcome of the JAG process.

To address the quality issue, the JAG sought to develop an industry standard that members would have to meet. Achieving this meant that members had to agree on an appropriate standard and develop a quality assurance certification programme. The JAG established a registered trademark, Australia Oat Hay, with its distinctive logo, which members would be entitled to use after having achieved quality certification. At the time of interviews, only one processor had completed the programme. The trademark formed an important part of the JAG's promotional campaign in Japan, and was officially launched during the group's Japanese trade mission in June 1994.

Out of the original ten members, two withdrew during the first two years of the JAG's operation–one of whom maintained contacts with some of the group. This same individual remarked: "If Australia Hay is successful . . . we would probably [re]join." Another processor, who attended the initial JAG formation meeting but elected not to join, made a similar comment, expressing concern that Japanese clients may come to recognise the logo and insist that all Australian exports conform to this standard.

The effect of the JAG's operations on market outcomes in Japan is difficult to judge at this stage. While there was a large increase in Australian oaten hay exports to Japan in 1993-1994, it would be difficult to attribute much of this to JAG activities, which were in the formative stages. Subsequently, the situation was overwhelmed by the severe drought, which slashed exports from the affected states.

China Grain

As the objective of the JAG was to assist in positioning Australian companies for possible design and construction work in the large China Grain project, in contrast to the Hay JAG, foreign market promotional activities were a major part of this JAG's operation. To this end, two trade missions to China were conducted in 1993, and JAG members, in conjunction with Austrade, hosted various delegations from Chinese grain agencies and government departments. These inward missions enabled JAG members to demonstrate their grain handling and storage capabilities.

The early phase could be described as selling Australia Incorporated. Promotional work in China was assisted by the appointment of a JAG-funded, dedicated Chinese marketing officer in Beijing, who worked in conjunction with Austrade's Beijing office. This marketing officer assisted with trade missions, relationship-building with appropriate Chinese agencies, and identification and selection of potential joint venture partners. As well, the Washington Austrade office liaised with relevant staff within the World Bank headquarters, and supported a World Bank official visit to meet JAG members. Such exposure helped in the appointment of a JAG member to the supervisory panel overseeing the China Grain project. Taken together, these activities raised the Australian profile, and assisted in ensuring JAG involvement in design work: one JAG member was appointed as the coordinating consultant for the detailed design work for one region, winning about 70% of the business.

The JAG was eventually disbanded, after the first release of construction tenders. Due to the drawn out nature of the pre-tender phase, many member companies had withdrawn from the JAG; or were inactive, although maintaining links through the Project Manager and/or other JAG members. Two JAG-based consortia had formed–one led by the Australian Wheat Board, the other by one of the smaller JAG members–and were competitive bidders for relevant project work. It was considered that the JAG had fulfilled its purpose and that it was an appropriate time to wind up the JAG's operations.

GROUPING ISSUES

Based on the investigation of both JAGs, a number of issues emerged that highlight the value and challenges of a more demand-driven approach to export grouping schemes. The following section examines these issues, with particular emphasis on aspects connected with group functioning and performance, including the role of the external facilitator.

Importance of Group Purpose

Given its previous experiences with various forms of export promotion schemes, the relevant officers within Austrade considered that having a strong foreign market goal would help to overcome the inherent problems with group operations (such as conflicting interests, personality clashes, lack of cohesion, etc.). Research has shown that an export group can be overwhelmed by individual concerns, even before any foreign market activities have begun–despite complementarity of group composition (Welch and Joynt, 1987). While studies of group goal-setting and performance are not as extensive as the research into that of individuals, there is evidence that group goals have a positive effect on outcomes. In their review of the literature, O'Leary-Kelly, Martocchio and Frink concluded: "95 percent of the studies that clearly used specific goals yielded positive results, but only 50 percent of those that did not clarify goal specificity did so" (1994, p. 1294). One could argue that the JAG principle incorporates goal-setting in a highly specific form, thus aiding group performance.

China Grain

Of course, within any group, several goals exist simultaneously: it is not only the superordinate group goal that applies, but also individual members' own goals–for themselves as well as the group. Because of these potentially conflicting goals, specificity is critically important to the group goal effect (Katzenbach and Smith, 1993; O'Leary-Kelly et al., 1994). Inevitably, Austrade had broad trade promotion goals, thus the Australia Incorporated strategy for the China Grain project, whereas individual companies were seeking their own specific outcomes. As one interviewee remarked:

> The idea of selling Australia first is a great way to go. Australia Incorporated sounds terrific but the individual companies don't want to sell Australia, they want to sell their products.

Nevertheless, with China Grain, there was clear compatibility in these goals in that the Chinese government agencies involved favoured a coordinated approach. This, plus the sheer magnitude of the project itself, added to the strength of the group goal effect. According to one JAG member:

> This project is large enough so that even for competitors there are enough opportunities . . . this is a far bigger problem in smaller projects.

Within such a large and variable group, there was naturally considerable divergence in the individual goals sought by JAG members, apart from the overall goal of winning project business. For example, for some smaller JAG members, exposure to the Chinese market was an important reason for joining the group. For companies with a history of Chinese operations, this was not an issue. In addition, some smaller companies clearly saw the JAG as an opportunity to network with experienced, major industry players. When asked why he joined the JAG, one member commented:

> To look at opportunities and network with members. Wanted contacts, to be part of the network they had put together.

Another member related:

> Obviously to get into China is a very costly exercise, especially for a company of this size. It [the JAG] provided an opportunity whereby for a minimum outlay we could reap the benefits of a much bigger approach into that market and we could receive the benefits of more experienced exporters' knowledge and abilities.

These companies were equipment suppliers and were dependent on joining with construction firms in a consortium. In this sense, they relied on the large companies winning a share of the China Grain project. One such large construction firm had eleven years of experience in China. During an interview, when discussing the tendering process, this JAG member pointed out:

> The smaller companies that are realistic know that they can only be successful through large companies like us . . . A ring from them now would be a nuisance. They know that if we need someone we will remember them.

Thus, JAG members tended to stress the inter-connectness of individual and JAG outcomes.

Over the life of the China Grain JAG, the number of financial members gradually declined. This was to be expected as companies clarified the opportunities available for them in the project. As one former JAG member explained:

> That is just a commercial reality–not a lot of obvious benefit for us.

Many of the smaller company members that withdrew expressed frustration at the constant delays associated with the project, and uncertainty about the nature of opportunities for them. It appeared from the interview data that the market opportunity had become a more nebulous goal, and other factors such as the cost of membership, tendering for other projects, etc., began to assume more importance. As research has shown, over time an intact group is likely to be influenced by many factors other than the group's goal (O'Leary-Kelly et al., 1994). Nevertheless, even these companies maintained connections with the JAG through networking (other members and Austrade), indicating that the market opportunity maintained its attraction, thus the group goal effect was still operative. For example, a former member, representing a training and consulting firm, noted:

> We are still looking at it [the project]. I have had talks with the Australian Wheat Board [a JAG member] about training opportunities.

Hay JAG

The underlying purpose of this JAG was to address a generally perceived problem of Australian supply instability–in quality, consistency and volume–typified by the action of one processor who had dumped a large quantity of substandard hay onto the Japanese market without prior sale. One JAG member, who withdrew about 18 months after the group's formation, explained:

> Probably the original reason for coming together as a group, unanimous I believe among the group, was to prevent this substandard hay being put in the market . . . We had a damn good business in Japan and overnight it went right out.

Such incidents were seen as hurting the reputation of all suppliers. In interviews, hay processors expressed concern about maintaining order in their relationships with Japanese clients, and their general reputation in the marketplace. For example:

> [The Jag was] basically to stop those cowboys. That was the aim of the exercise at the end of the day–to force them out of the market. This meant getting the industry to work as one.

This [the JAG] was one way of possibly getting around that [instability problem], by getting a cohesive group together and discussing prices and discussing quality.

Market protection therefore was the primary goal of the JAG members. This required co-ordinated effort in such areas as the development of an industry standard, and joint market promotion, as well as enhanced information flows between members. As with the China Grain JAG, Austrade had the broader goal of increasing oaten hay exports to Japan. This, however, tended to be of secondary concern for individual hay processors. It was seen more as an outcome of dealing with the instability issue, with many JAG members regarding their market position as satisfactory. It should be noted here that the hay processors were reliant on their supplies of hay from a network of local farmers and had to convince them to conform to processor standards.

Individual members continued to market their own hay in Japan, and to develop closer relationships with their domestic hay suppliers. It would appear though that, over time, as members began to identify with the JAG, they developed a stronger commitment to the goals of the group. There appeared to be implicit recognition that, though they were head-to-head competitors, achievement of the common purpose of improving quality would result in improved individual positions. The Hay JAG's Project Manager, when interviewed in September 1994, considered that the group had developed a sense of ownership, helped by joint JAG activities. This is in line with research on group dynamics, which indicates that it is common for members to identify more with the group as they become better acquainted with each other. Interaction increases, information exchange occurs, and "a rudimentary level of trust develops" (Forsyth, 1990, p. 78).

From the case analysis, an important variable was the time span between group formation and achievement of outcomes. The China Grain experience demonstrates that the longer the period between group formation and achievement of tangible results, the greater the difficulty in keeping group members focused, thus weakening the group goal effect. The Hay JAG members were better placed to undertake the initiatives required in addressing the primary group goal, and therefore had more of a sense of achievement at an early stage.

GROUP FUNCTIONING

The significance of the group goal effect that emerged during the evaluation appeared to validate the demand-driven approach of the JAG scheme. However, other factors inherent in group functioning played an important role in terms of group performance in the two JAGs investigated. These included group composition, group size and group cohesion.

Group Composition

In contrast to supply-driven approaches (Welch and Joynt, 1987; Luostarinen et al., 1994) where group composition tends to be more carefully controlled in the formation phase, to a large extent, membership of both JAGs could be described as self-selected. The first meeting to form the Hay JAG included all the major processors who had been invited by Austrade. However, there was an element of control in that potential members were strongly opposed to one particular processor and ensured he was not included. This individual's operations were regarded as representing the problem that led to the perceived need for the JAG. There was no attempt to control membership in the China Grain JAG. On the contrary, partly due to the nature of the project, and the Australia Incorporated approach, the strategy was to attract all relevant industry participants. This reflected the demand-driven approach in that the focus was on a specific opportunity as a way of motivating and pulling in relevant industry players. However, there is an inherent risk in this approach, given that there is no control over the compatibility of members: the experience of past schemes demonstrates that group composition is an important variable in determining outcomes (OECD, 1964; Welch and Joynt, 1987).

By its very nature, the Hay JAG was composed of companies who, to a greater or lesser extent, were competitors. The level of perceived competition was affected by location, as processors in similar growing areas appeared more concerned with each other than with processors from other regions or states. However, competition between the processors did not emerge as a serious problem in the group's operations. The competitive urge tended to be moderated by the sense of common purpose, the positive benefits of improved intra-group communication, and joint activities such as the quality assurance programme. For example, one Hay JAG member commented:

> To think that the group was actually started–it could have fallen
> by the wayside simply because we are competitors. It has helped
> us [his firm] to be able to talk to these other people. We as a
> group have got this immense marketing information that we can
> use together. We can exchange information.

Despite co-operation, competitive activities between Hay JAG members did not cease. However, the intra-group conflict that occurred seemed to be occasioned more by personality clashes and differences of opinion than by competitive action. Of the original ten members who formed the Hay JAG, two had withdrawn at the time of interviews, one of whom was the largest hay exporter to the Japanese market. This processor had a strong personality with strong views about the direction and purpose of the JAG, and thus put him at odds with some JAG members. As Forsyth argues: "Interdependency among members and the stability of a group cannot deepen until intragroup hostility has surfaced, been confronted, and resolved" (1990, p. 385). In interviews, other JAG members expressed regret at his withdrawal, but his absence did not appear to adversely affect group functioning. Personality clashes are not unexpected behavioural outcomes of group interaction: even with considered selection of members, it is difficult to predict personal compatibility. In a way, the exiting of this strong individual was typical of normal group processes: as part of what is termed "the storming stage" of group development, where roles, norms and leadership are established as a prelude to more settled and ordered group activity (Robbins, 1986, pp. 172-173).

Group Size

The demand-driven approach appeared to lead to a de-emphasis on the question of group size, as there appeared to be little or no consideration of this factor during the formation of either JAG. Rather, the aim was to attract all of the major players in both cases. Research, however, shows that the larger the group the harder it is to manage (Barney and Griffin, 1992). The larger size of the China Grain JAG seemed to create a more demanding managerial task compared with the Hay JAG. Robbins argues that "groups of approximately seven members tend to be more effective for action taking" (1986, p. 190). In the export grouping context, it has long been recognised "that the possibility of disagreement increases with the number of co-operating firms" (OECD, 1964, p. 22).

The heterogeneity of China Grain JAG members in terms of firm size, nature of business, international and Chinese experience, and the mix of complementarity and competitiveness, increased the likelihood of conflict rather than co-operation. In this large group, the openness in group composition meant that potential competitive behaviour existed at two levels: first, there were members who were direct competitors in supplying equipment and services. As one China Grain JAG member remarked:

> The market focus is extremely important in this operation. On the negative side, the fact that you get occasionally personality clashes and the like . . . clashes are between firms doing similar things.

Second, there was an inherent capacity to form sub-groups, or consortia, who could bid against each other for the same project work. In fact, within the first year of operation, the Australian Wheat Board formed a consortium as a basis for ultimate bidding for the construction work. This included two large construction firms (one non-JAG) and 50 other companies, not all of whom were JAG members. While this caused conflict over the roles of Austrade and the Australian Wheat Board that was eventually settled at government ministerial level it did not spill over to JAG operations. Although research has shown that role conflict within groups can produce negative consequences for performance (Barney and Griffin, 1992), the effect here was minimal: JAG members interviewed tended to regard it as a side issue, an internal government problem. The only concern was that it might adversely affect the JAG's promotional activity in China. Those members interviewed who were part of the Australian Wheat Board's consortium saw their involvement as only an informal arrangement. When tenders were finally released, two JAG-based consortia entered competitive bids. Even though this was always seen as a potential outcome, once the rival camps became a reality in the marketplace, it became a trigger in the disbandment of the China Grain JAG. By this stage there appeared to be a consensus that the JAG's role had been completed.

Group Cohesion

One explanation for the limited impact that the above composition factors had on group cohesion is that many members had what could be described as passive involvement. These passive members were waiting for the issue of tenders and the constant delays dampened both enthusiasm and competitiveness. One could suggest that the thinning of ranks caused by withdrawals also assisted. In a sense, they were in a hiatus in which they were not engaged in direct competitive activity. A further moderating factor was the structure of the JAG: as a company, it was run by a Board of Directors comprising seven JAG members, and Austrade was represented at the meetings. The Board, in many ways, was the JAG. It made all important decisions. This small inner circle met frequently, whereas the JAG as a whole did not have formal meetings, only getting together as the various foreign delegations visited Australia. The Company Secretary commented that the Board "functioned reasonably well." It was composed of non-competitive members, although there were some, non-disruptive, personality clashes. As one Board member observed:

> [The] Board was very diverse. Some on Board who didn't like each other . . . did not stop us working co-operatively.

Group dynamics research has shown that conflict can actually promote group unity, provided that it does not escalate. Forsyth notes: "Conflict also preserves a group by providing a means of venting interpersonal hostilities" (1990, p. 385).

By contrast, the Hay JAG was a small, relatively homogeneous group. As one member described it: "we are all country town [and] like a beer." The oaten hay processors were strong-minded, independent individuals, with a somewhat common negative attitude towards lawyers, consultants and academics, expressed in interviews with such comments as: "far too much use of consultants." Psychological and management research into small group behaviour has shown that similar attitudes, experience and demographic backgrounds assist in group cohesiveness–although this does not guarantee high performance (Jackson, 1992). Cohesiveness was assisted by a level of awareness of each other prior to JAG formation, with some members already in contact with each other.

THE ROLE OF THE EXTERNAL FACILITATOR

According to Bayer, "co-operative producer networks do not in general arise spontaneously" (1994, p. 10). Similarly, without the intervention of Austrade, it is doubtful that either of the JAGs would have come into existence. Further, Austrade played a critical role in keeping the JAGs operational and market focused. This was confirmed in interviews, with statements such as:

Hay JAG Members:

. . . if they [Austrade] had not put the group together it would not have got off the ground.

Austrade got us together and contacted these people [other government agencies] about funds, ran the secretariat, which helped us survive.

China Grain JAG Members:

[Austrade] are the catalyst and they held it [the JAG] together for a long time . . . if Austrade had pulled out, the group would probably have fallen apart.

If it weren't for Austrade as a catalyst, the whole thing would have fallen apart by now.

Austrade and the JAG are the focal point for a lot of the correspondence and relationships that are happening in the industry . . . so they are playing an extremely important role. They are just facilitating really well.

One explanation of Austrade's ability to play this role as catalyst could be that, because of its charter to assist Australian exporters, it had "bona fide intentions from the perception of the group's participants" (Welch, 1992, p. 23). In interviews, some members from both JAGs referred to previous attempts that had been made by companies, in response to perceived market concerns, to establish similar groupings. These initiatives appeared to fail due to group internal competitiveness and the lack of direction from an acceptable group leader or facilitator. As one China Grain JAG member recalled with regard to an earlier grouping effort:

> We had a lot of difficulty because there was the competitive issue . . . the notion of having a group was good but how to make it work was a problem . . . really it did not work.

For each JAG, an Austrade officer was appointed to act as Project Manager. Both JAG Project Managers were involved from the pre-formation stage: assisting in identifying potential group members, and organising the initial public meetings. They then performed a secretarial role for the JAGs, organised trade missions, and assisted in market promotion activities. The Project Managers played a major information clearing house role: generating, assembling and disseminating JAG relevant information from a wide variety of sources, both within Australia and in each of the target markets (and in the case of China Grain, the World Bank in New York). They also acted as a conduit between the JAG and key government agencies and industry groups. For example, a Hay JAG member stated:

> [Project Manager] was very good and we would not have kept together without her.

Similar comments were made by China Grain members:

> [Project Manager] keeps the JAG together, gets people there . . . this has been particularly difficult given the lack of a concrete timeframe.
>
> . . . Project Manager was critical. Co-ordination was essential.

Interview data also showed that, over time, each Project Manager was perceived by individual JAG members as being "our person in Austrade" who could assist in various matters, including those not specifically related to JAG activities. This level of trust and ownership allowed these Project Managers to bring about a higher level of influence than otherwise would have been the case, and gave them some ability to steer the groups. Their activity appeared to complement rather than counter the role of the Board in each case, who in fact came to rely on the Project Managers.

There was some difference between the two JAGs regarding the role of the Project Manager over time. To some extent, dependence on the China Grain Project Manager increased because of the nature of the project and the delay in the issuance of tenders. This was perhaps most evident among the JAG members who either became passive or withdrew; the Project Manager became the key link back to the JAG. As one former JAG member commented:

> I would hope that [Project Manager] when something concrete comes up, would tell us JAG members past and present that there is something for us.

In contrast, Hay JAG members were prepared to lessen their dependency on the Project Manager as they developed informal links between each other and confidence about their ability to direct the group's operations. Nevertheless, they clearly saw the advantages of maintaining and using the Austrade link. As one member explained:

> Now it [the JAG] is running properly, we only meet twice a year. All the work has been done, the company set up and running properly as a legal entity. It is not as big a job as it was previously but Austrade should maintain an involvement.

This perspective was illustrated by their reaction to the early withdrawal of Austrade from the JAG. Only fifteen months after its formation, an outside secretariat, a small legal firm, was appointed to replace the Austrade Project Manager. The arrangement was entered into somewhat reluctantly by the JAG members and lasted for only nine months. During this period, the Austrade Project Manager held a watching brief, and was still consulted by JAG members on a regular basis to solve problems–even to the point of actually by-passing the official secretariat. As well, the Project Manager organised for the group to undertake a promotional mission to Japan. When the decision was taken by the JAG to sever the connection with the legal firm, it renegotiated an agreement with Austrade on a cost-recovery basis, using the part-time services of one of its staff to continue the secretarial role. Having a direct connection to Austrade was considered important: the external secretariat was perceived to be at a disadvantage as it did not have the inside knowledge and contacts to expedite JAG concerns.

Thus, the Project Manager became more a co-leader than an external facilitator (Forsyth, 1990). In the Hay JAG, the Project Manager initiated many of the group activities and appeared to be important in maintaining focus on market goal achievement. For example, she initiated the exploration of other foreign market opportunities for the JAG and subsequently decided that these alternatives were inappropriate:

> . . . we were planning to go to Korea and Taiwan. . . . but I initiated some research beforehand and the markets were not looking too good short term, so I made the decision not to go ahead with the visits.

This occurred in 1994 when Austrade had formally handed over the secretariat role and the Project Manager was only performing a "support" function. Likewise, the China Grain Project Manager described himself as playing a "middle manager role," although the interview data revealed that because of the infrequent meetings of JAG members and the reliance of the Board on him, he effectively had more influence on the direction and operation of the JAG. Thus, in both JAGs, the Project Managers developed into a position that could be described as co-leadership. While having the potential to be dysfunctional, such joint leadership was positive for the group because of what the Project Managers were contributing: expertise, government contacts, knowledge, etc.

In summary, Austrade performed a critical role in group formation and maintenance. Initially, it was the catalyst and, over time, its Project Managers assumed broader task roles (Forsyth, 1990, p. 112). These evolved to be more than just facilitation: including steering, information collection and dissemination, networking, and marketing. Such activities contributed to the development of group cohesion, communication between members, and conflict resolution; they helped to keep each JAG focused on the market goal.

IMPLICATIONS

The above analysis and discussion of a new Australian demand-driven export grouping scheme provides insights into the benefits of this approach, but also into the range of associated requirements if such schemes are to fulfil their potential. The experience of the two JAGs seems to confirm the impact of the group goal effect on group performance shown in organisational behaviour research. The market goal appeared to have had a positive effect on group functioning.

However, grouping issues were still found to be important. Both JAGs showed evidence of problems caused by large size (as in the China Grain JAG), personality clashes, and competitive behaviour, which might well have overwhelmed each operation, thus negating the group goal effect. That they did not is perhaps an indication of the strength of the goal effect, and the critical role played by the Project Managers in keeping the JAGs focused on the market opportunity. Based on the JAG experience, we would argue that once a market goal has been established as appropriate for group action, it is necessary to address market goal attainment and group functioning in tandem, as shown in Figure 3. Keeping this dual concern is, however, difficult. The demands of group formation and maintenance can become a distraction from the ultimate purpose of the exercise. Likewise, ignoring grouping issues can result in failure (Stenberg, 1982). Group dynamics research has shown that "few groups are productive immedi-

FIGURE 3. Market Development and Grouping Activities

ately; instead, productivity must usually wait until the group matures" (Forsyth, 1990, p. 85). Inevitably, the supporters of such schemes tend to be impatient for early results.

Stressing the goal as the reason for the group's existence inevitably places prominence on its achievement, so that there must be evidence that group actions are leading to its attainment. In other words, members need tangible evidence that commitment to the group is worthwhile (Forsyth, 1990). For example, the China Grain JAG experienced substantial withdrawal of members due to frustration over the delay in the issue of tenders. Initially, group activity to sell Australian expertise, involving the organisation of trade missions to China, and hosting Chinese visits to Australia, were tangible steps along the way to goal achievement. Once this burst of activity ceased for the majority, with no concrete results, the perceived market opportunity diminished and other concerns assumed importance. For the Hay JAG, though, the need to establish an industry standard naturally lent itself to subgoals: establishing the quality standard, registering the trademark and launching the logo in Japan, and undergoing the necessary quality certification process. This appeared to provide the group with the necessary sense of achievement, supported by the increased group contact and its benefits (such as price information, and knowledge sharing). As shown in Figure 3, in a broader sense, one may argue that demand-driven export grouping schemes should be structured in such a way as to allow for the achievement of subgoals as soon as possible. One positive aspect of setting a time constraint on Austrade's involvement was that it forced members to think about the purpose of the group rather than perceiving the group as an end in itself.

Figure 3 also includes a group facilitator position, based on the role played by Project Managers in the two JAGs. As discussed above, the Project Manager was a key reference point for each JAG. They appeared to be important in ensuring that an "in-tandem" approach was feasible, as they were heavily involved in both market goal achievement and group formation and maintenance activities. The resistance to early exit by Austrade is indicative of how JAG members perceived this contribution. Given the significance of the position, the appointment of the group facilitator should perhaps assume more importance in the development of such export grouping schemes.

The research reported in this article is based on the experience of only two groups within a new demand-driven export grouping scheme over a relatively short time span. Clearly, this research needs to be extended, by examination of other, similar schemes, on a more widespread basis and to assess their effects over a longer period: to see whether the groups are able to maintain productive, co-operative activity, and how group processes evolve and affect outcomes in the longer term.

REFERENCES

Barney, J.B. and R.W. Griffin (1992), *The Management of Organisations: Strategy, Structure, Behavior*, Boston: Houghton Mifflin Company.

Bayer, K. (1994), "Co-operative Small-Firm Networks as Factors in Regional Industrial Development," Occasional Paper No. 48, European Free Trade Association, Geneva, July.

Cavusgil, S.T. and M.R. Czinkota, eds. (1990), *International Perspectives on Trade Promotion and Assistance*, New York: Quorum Books.

Department of Foreign Affairs and Trade (1995), *Winning Enterprises*, Canberra: Australian Government Publishing Service.

Ferris, W.D., ed. (1985), *Lifting Australia's Performance as an Exporter of Manufactures and Services*, Canberra: Australian Government Printing Service.

Forsyth, D.R. (1990), *Group Dynamics*, 2nd edition, Pacific Grove, CA: Brooks/Cole Publishing Company.

Jackson, S.E. (1992), "Consequences of Group Composition for the Interpersonal Dynamics of Strategic Issue Processing," *Advances in Strategic Management* 8, pp. 345-82.

Katzenbach, J.R. and D.K. Smith (1993), "The Discipline of Teams," *Harvard Business Review* 71 (2), pp. 111-19.

Kedia, B.L. and J.S. Chhokar (1986), "An Empirical Investigation of Export Promotion Programs," *Columbia Journal of World Business* 21 (4), pp. 13-20.

Luostarinen, R., H. Korhonen, J. Jokinen and T. Pelkonen (1994), *Globalisation and SME*, Study and Report No. 59, Helsinki: Ministry of Trade and Industry, Finland.

Nothdurft, W.E. (1992), *Going Global: How Europe Helps Small Firms Export*, Washington: The Brookings Institution.

OECD (1964), *Export Marketing Groups for Small and Medium-Sized Firms*, Paris.

O'Leary-Kelly, A.M, J.J. Martocchio, and D.D. Frink (1994), "A Review of The Influence of Group Goals on Group Performance," *Academy of Management Journal* 37 (5) pp. 1285-1301.

Patton, M.Q. (1990), *Qualitative Evaluation and Research Methods*, Newbury Park, CA: Sage Publications.

Robbins, S.P. (1986), *Organizational Behavior: Concepts, Controversies, and Applications*, 2nd edition, New York: Prentice Hall International.

Seringhaus, R. and P.J. Rosson, eds. (1990), *Government Export Promotion: A Global Perspective*, London: Routledge.

Stake, R.E. (1994), "Case Studies," in N.K. Denzin and Y.S. Lincoln, eds., *Handbook of Qualitative Research*, Thousand Oaks: Sage Publications, pp. 236-47.

Stenberg, T. (1982), *System Co-operation: A Possibility for Swedish Industry*, Department of Business Administration, University of Goteborg.

Strandell, A.C. (1985), "Export Co-operation–Company Experience," delivered at The European International Business Association Conference, Glasgow, December 15-17.

Van de Ven, A.H. (1976), "On the Nature, Formation and Maintenance of Relations Among Organizations," *Academy of Management Review* 1 (4), pp. 24-36.

Welch, D., L.S. Welch, I. Wilkinson and L. Young (1996), "Network Analysis of a New Export Grouping Scheme: The Role of Economic and Non-Economic Relations," *International Journal of Research in Marketing* 13 (5), pp. 463-77.

Welch, L.S. (1992). "The Use of Alliances by Small Firms in Achieving Internationalization," *Scandinavian International Business Review* 1 (2), pp. 21-37.

Welch, L.S. and P. Joynt (1987), "Grouping for Export: An Effective Solution?" in P.J. Rosson and S.D. Reid, eds., *Managing Export Entry and Expansion: Concepts and Practice*, New York: Praeger, pp. 54-70.

Yin, R.K. (1994), *Case Study Research: Design and Methods*, Newbury Park, CA: Sage Publications.

International Competition
and Global Co-Operation

Frank L. Bartels

SUMMARY. This paper exposes emerging issues that form a robust platform for the integration of two asymmetric, but archetypal, forms of 21st century business organisation responsible for wealth creation at the global and local level–Multi-Transnational Enterprises (MTNEs) and Small and Medium Enterprises (SMEs). It does so in the context of the business environment increasingly characterised by a complex dynamic of change among firms that is a change from international competition to global co-operation. The paper considers the major implications of the geo-economically dispersed but Integrated International Sourcing, Production and Marketing Networks (IISPMNs) of MTNEs and examines issues for the engagement of SMEs in the resulting information processing and knowledge creation. It concludes by delineating the dimensions of this engagement which form a hitherto insufficiently researched business agenda. *[Article copies available for a fee from The Haworth Document Delivery Service: 1-800-342-9678. E-mail address: <getinfo@haworthpressinc.com> Website: <http://www.HaworthPress.com>]*

KEYWORDS. SMEs, co-operation, integration, internationalisation

INTRODUCTION

The essential purpose of any firm is to maintain a posture that expresses strategic coherence in its competitive and co-operative rela-

Frank L. Bartels is affiliated with the Nanyang Business School, Singapore.

[Haworth co-indexing entry note]: "International Competition and Global Co-Operation." Bartels, Frank L. Co-published simultaneously in *Journal of Euromarketing* (International Business Press, an imprint of The Haworth Press, Inc.) Vol. 9, No. 2, 2000, pp. 85-97; and: *Global Marketing Co-Operation and Networks* (ed: Leo Paul Dana) International Business Press, an imprint of The Haworth Press, Inc., 2000, pp. 85-97. Single or multiple copies of this article are available for a fee from The Haworth Document Delivery Service [1-800-342-9678, 9:00 a.m. - 5:00 p.m. (EST). E-mail address: getinfo@haworthpressinc.com].

tions with economic structures in both its immediate and near industrial supply and market demand environments. Global economic development vectors indicate that the creation and maintenance of strategic coherence for businesses is becoming increasingly difficult for firms, big and small, in the light of major shifts in industrial organisation, the market and technology. The major challenge to contemporary business is accepting twin notions that firstly, spatial and temporal constraints are no longer significant as barriers and secondly, that the morphology of *what is a business* is defined less and less by the physical characteristics of output and products. From a technological perspective products are becoming "less material, more abstract." Access to information (data imbued with purpose), its creation and management is increasingly the differentiating factor between business success and failure. "This means that the world is becoming more 'abstract,' more 'immaterial'. . . . In the formation of value, it is more and more difficult to localize its material components. And value is based on the capacity to be accessed" (Guéhenno, 1995, p. 8). These shifts represent a new economic era, or paradigm, and may be designated–the age of network capitalism or the knowledge-based economy (Thurow, 1999). The impact for marketing is profound and the implications of the changes pose serious challenges for smaller firms from both developed and developing countries as they attempt to engage with the global economy. The ensuing requirements for strategic coherence provide a rich agenda for business organisation research that hitherto has not received the kind of attention it deserves.

The stylised set of issues in international business and strategy concern the key unit of analysis–Multi-Transnational Enterprises (MTNEs). Research implications regarding Small and Medium Enterprises (SMEs) that emerge from the MTNEs' attempt to cohere strategically spatially dispersed and differentiated features of their international organisation, constitute an emerging agenda. More and more firms are becoming connected globally through formal and informal relations that do not clearly represent either market or contract mechanisms or even "concrete" relations. One major implication is that an accurate understanding of determinants and dimensions of the multi-national management of spatially dispersed and differentiated but temporally unified organisations assists in the SMEs' engagement with global capitalism.

The features of globalisation since its onset (circa 1973/74) have been defined by ever increasing, deepening and widening flows of

Foreign Direct Investment (FDI) and Foreign Portfolio Investment (FPI). In a symbiotic convergent dynamic FDI has generated profitable industrial inter-linkages, with valuable market outputs, worthy of portfolio interest. In turn, FPI has brought the vanguard of venture capital and generated interest in investment in productive assets. However, it is becoming increasingly difficult to separate the two streams. It is within this convergence that SMEs require a means of engagement with MTNEs that delivers valuable returns.

THE GLOBAL MARKET
OF MULTI-TRANSNATIONAL ENTERPRISES

The relatively small number of MTNEs (between 50,000 and 60,000 with their approximately 450,000 subsidiaries between them) are directly responsible for 65% to 70% of global trade (UNCTAD, 1997). This comprises of inter-MTNEs revenue generating transactions and, more importantly for our purposes, intra-MTNEs exports and imports that occur within the geo-economic organisational boundaries of the firm without the intermediation of external factor markets. In recent years, particularly since the mid-1980s, the dominant form of business intermediation has moved significantly from one with an emphasis on international competition to one of cross-border co-operation–a process designated as alliance capitalism (Dunning, 1994/95). This new emphasis is leading to intensifying pressures for creating distributed inter-locking lattices for engaging "acquired" assets in ways that enable MTNEs to project, beyond their immediate vicinity, organisational and operational architectures that are torsionally flexible and immediately responsive.

This development is supported by two modes of dynamic evidence. The first is the inundation of inward FDI not only to the triad of developed regions but also to the Emerging Markets (EMs) particularly of South East Asia and which are held partly responsible for the "event horizon" of the Asian Economic Crisis that erupted in mid-1997. Global in-FDI multiplied steadily from below US$150 B in 1991 to a record total of US$400 B in 1997 before expanding by a massive 39% to US$644 B by end-1998 (UNCTAD, 1999) having dipped in early-1998 in response to the recession in Asia. The second constellation of evidence is the unprecedented scale in the volume and value, and scope of the variety of cross-border inter-firm formal and informal relations collectively termed conveniently as Joint International Business Associations (JIBAs). JIBAs encapsulate Mergers and Acquisitions (MAs), International Joint Ventures (IJVs), International Strategic Alliances (ISAs), as well as Technology and Marketing Agreements (TMAs).

Several realities of the unprecedented rise in JIBAs are inherent in the maturing industrial sectors of agri-business, auto-aerospace, banking-finance, electronics, food-beverage, petro-chemicals, pharmaceuticals and telecommunications. In these industries, the overriding pressures are to secure economies of scale followed by highly selective applications of economies of scope using key industry drivers. For example in agri-business, bio-genetics are the key technology driver; in auto-aerospace, advanced composite materials are the key technology driver; in electronics, silicon nano-technology is the key driver; and in pharmaceuticals, genome technology is the key driver. Consequently, cross-border MAs sales totaled US$342 B in 1997 (World Bank, 1999) and constituted 60%, or US$240 B, of all 1997 in-FDI. This is an increase from 30%, or US$45 B, of 1991 in-FDI.

The dynamics in intra-industry competitiveness (Porter, 1990) point to increased proportions of in-FDI being effected through MAs. Between 1996 and 1998 there were over 20,000 ISAs formed worldwide. ISAs deliver an increasing share of MTNEs' revenues amounting to about 21%, double what it was in the early 1990s. This trend is likely to accelerate over the next few years as competitive pressures build up and force MTNEs to behave more oligopolistically. Already since the beginning of 1999, over 10,400 firms have announced MAs valued at over US$1.2 T. The number of bio-technology ISAs for the leading 20 pharmaceutical MTNEs alone have increased dramatically from 152 in the period 1988-90 to 375 in 1997-98 and the number of inter-firm technology and marketing agreements has also increased from 280 during 1980-83 to 650 in 1996 alone. This represents a 132% increase in activity. The regional and international dimensions to these figures are provided by two facts: (a) between the first and second halves of 1997, Singapore-based regional headquarters of MTNEs increased their MAs by 1280% from US$0.145 B to US$2.001 B (UNCTAD-ICC, 1998); and (b) 1998 being designated the year of the mega-merger with a total of US$563 B between just nine pairs of MTNEs (Colvin, 1999).

Bartels and Mirza (1999) provide a further measure of this global dynamic within the context of rising global FDI and intra-regional trade that have asymmetric distributions. Between 1980 and 1996 the stock of world FDI increased from about US$514 B to around US$3,233 B. Hence the global reach of MTNEs and their JIBAs, represented by stocks of FDI, carry implications for industrial organisation and the management of enterprise that are presently at the nascent stage of definition and formation.

THE LITERATURE AND ITS LACUNAE

Issues implicit in the realisation that international firms are increasingly spatially distributed collections of symbiotically active centres (displaying inherently contending forces) of data and information processing, and knowledge and competence creation, have not been fully addressed. In particular, international business, strategic and marketing literature on co-operative forms of industrial organisation is wanting. There are exceptions.

Conner (1991) provides a valuable basis for scrutinising the international firm from the perspective of resources and addresses the historical antecedents of the theory of the firm. However, the resource-based literature presented is arguably short on explications for the morphology of inter-firm inter-facial relations in JIBAs. Spekman et al. (1998) deal with the contradiction inherent in the fact that the increase in JIBAs is mirrored by an increasing number of "failures" of the formal and informal relations at intra-organisational inter-faces. A number of contributors to the literature approach the issues of the shape of motivations that animate inter-organisation and intra-organisation inter-faces in terms of reductions in transactional costs and the efficiencies of hierarchical or market governance mechanisms (Sriram, Krapfel and Spekman, 1992; Larson, 1992). Others point to the dichotomy of the security of total control from full ownership and the contested benefits of shared access to extra-firm specific advantages (Teece, 1992; Borys and Jemison, 1989). However, the emergent issue of "communications, co-ordination, control and command of inter-facing" is scantily addressed.

Recently Cohendet et al. (1999) argued that for MTNEs, the priorities of managing the purposeful unequal distribution of information, in order to keep high appropriabilities at the centre, has been replaced by those of leveraging and managing the mobilisation and integration of fragmented and dispersed forms of localised knowledge from the periphery of the organisation. However, the approach addresses inadequately the problem of autonomy and dependence in headquarter-subsidiary relationships. Although this lacuna is partly addressed by Antonelli (1999) with an approach to the industrial organisation of knowledge that focuses on the trade-off between forms of knowledge creation and "dissemination receptivity and connectivity," the problems faced by JIBAs are not fully explored as to their differentiation by location and socio-culture. The empirical evidence of Blanc and Sierra (1999) focuses on the trade-off between "internal and external proximity" within the internationalisation dynamics of MTNEs. In their focus, while the underlying platform of the eclectic paradigm of international production (Dunning, 1998) is propagated as the base explanation for JIBAs, the problem of managing the sub-contracting of technological innovation is not given central attention.

AN EMERGENT BUSINESS RESEARCH AGENDA

The research agenda identifiable as emergent transcends the international business, strategy and marketing literatures, and converges suggestively on an information-processing theory of MTNEs (Egelhoff, 1991). Received literature indicates that MTNEs have traditionally sought firstly to match organically developed Firm Specific Advantages (FSAs) with Location Specific Advantages (LSAs), such as technology with skilled but low-cost labour in developing countries; and secondly to distribute globally value-adding activities in such a manner as to ensure high appropriabilities, through IISPMNs, at source. Industrial organisation economic theory assists in understanding why firms should wish to achieve "costly to copy attributes." If firms cannot make such attributes, they purchase or co-opt them by internalising external factor markets. These factor markets may involve "hard" inputs (labour) or "soft" (political) inputs (Boddewyn and Brewer, 1994). Hence the phenomenal rise in JIBAs. The result of increased JIBAs is even more global dispersal of intra-organisational functions, not only in terms of mandates but also of local repositories of technical know-how and competence. Furthermore, the majority of this capacity and associated capability to create knowledge is tacit.

What is critical for today's MTNEs is ensuring intra-organisational access to this tacit material. Such intra-organisational access implies less emphasis on means for deliberate unequal distribution of knowledge and a much greater accent, within JIBAs, on mechanisms for accessing, integrating and circulating diversified treasuries of local competence throughout the organisation for increasing leverage and competitiveness. By way of illustration, one example of diversified treasuries–the innovative Kodak product "Kodakcolour Gold" was created by Kodak Japan, not Kodak USA. In the bio-tech industries the race to acquire nascent SMEs, those showing a potential for patenting winning formulations that has fuelled industry concentration, is driven partly by these same pressures.

With increasing cross-border JIBAs, decisions as to what is done where, by who and to what extent within MTNEs grow in importance. The strategic implication for international business is a move from "planning" to "projecting" mirrored by a move from organisational hierarchy to business heterarchy. Systematically, international firms have centralised the orchestration of non-market functions (e.g., fiscal and treasury operations, finance and budgeting) to increase economies of scale efficiencies while decentralising the co-ordination of market functions (e.g., product adaptation and promotion) to enhance effectiveness and customer responsiveness and thereby increase competitiveness. However, this first order spatial integration may no longer be sufficient as shown by recent evidence from a second order spatial integration undertaken by Caltex. Caltex has re-organised its entire network so that particular subsidiaries in specific locations perform certain defined operations. Globally, Caltex financial and treasury operations remain the mandate of the Houston subsidiary; products and development, sales, marketing and distribution operations are the responsibility of the Singapore global headquarters; organisational information and communications technology and computing are conveyed by the subsidiary in South Africa; the subsidiary in Bangkok is responsible for all firm training; and the subsidiary in Kuala Lumpur runs all credit based operations. All nodes are integrated and related by information and communications technology.

These developments and requirements beg the question of how increasingly dispersed MTNEs (that is, decreasing organisational densities) achieve "strategic coherence" (that is, high-density performance). In other words, how does executive management ensure that acquired and added but globally distributed knowledge-intense assets are effectively and efficiently shared throughout the organisation?

This question, oriented to the SMEs which, inter-linked with the MTNEs to form further distributed assets, delivers a rich vein for international business and strategy research to explore.

It is suggested that four broad dimensions delimit the emergent research domain for managing "strategic coherence" at the global level: corporate culture, subsidiary mandates, treasury, and intra-organisational inter-faces. The first dimension–managing corporate culture–has features that arise from collective legacies and corporate memory and therefore imbue it with a co-operative orientation. This in turn gives rise to centripetal forces inside the dispersed (low density) organisation. The second dimension–managing subsidiary mandates–has a competitive orientation. After all, it is competition between the subsidiaries of the MTNEs' JIBAs that discloses which subsidiary is best able to perform a particular function or operation. This in turn gives rise to centrifugal forces within the dispersed organisation. The third dimension–managing intra-organisational inter-faces–has a maximising orientation in so far as effectiveness in sharing distributed localities of competence implies maximum levels of communications and co-ordination among the organisational nodes of the MTNEs. This gives rise to high contact intensities across the diffuse organisational boundaries. The fourth dimension–managing treasury operations–has an optimising orientation because of the fiscal and operational implications of international transfer pricing. This gives rise to forces of command and control across organisational boundaries.

IMPLICATIONS OF THE EMERGENT RESEARCH AGENDA

What then are the implications for research at the nascent stage of definition and formation that are relevant to SMEs and subsidiaries? These revolve around ascertaining determinants, quantifications and qualifications on the one hand, and, on the other hand, delineating the impacts of MTNEs networks and sub-contracting on SMEs and subsidiaries. Evidence suggests strongly that MTNEs are increasingly demonstrating an enhanced ability to leverage the echelons and quality of their multi-directional linkages. According to Guéhenno (1995, p. 60), "each unit of the enterprise must be sufficiently grounded in its local network fully to play its role of *receptor* vis-à-vis the 'outside' and be sufficiently 'linked' to the other units of the enterprise to act out fully its role as *distributor* within the company." This is entirely to do with the changing nature of information and knowledge, the value of which lies in exchange. Three major implications are evident.

The first implication is that the four dimensions that define the emergent research domain for managing "strategic coherence" at the global level are inherently contradictory or at least are described by vectors that are in dynamic opposition. This militates against coherence. The second implication is that management changes from control over deployment of resources and becomes intermediation–"constantly adjusting the organization of the relationships between the different units" in directing MTNEs (Guéhenno, 1995, p. 60). The third implication is that organisational power no longer resides in the possession of knowledge but in the efficient and effective operational link between centres of competence and nodes of knowledge.

Furthermore, the factors that delineate the research dimensions indicated above have yet to be either fully explored or modeled for confirmatory factor analysis. The factors that delineate the research dimension–managing intra-organisational corporate culture–comprise variables that concern leadership and corporate memory. Especially as it is recognised that human capital and its management is key to success in JIBAs. The findings of a seminal study by Spekman et al. (1996, p. 348) "demonstrate the inextricable linkage between the business of the alliance and the interpersonal relationship between the key alliance players." However, given the fact that one of the fundamental features of the knowledge-economy is of the absence of "careers" (Thurow, 1999), these leadership variables and questions revolve about issues that include: the extent to which management of human resources cohere with the need for flexibility in professional services; the extent to which the different cultural contexts of acquired assets moderate integration and sharing of dispersed sites of knowledge and competence; the challenge of diversity in MTNEs organisational behaviours; and the challenges of leadership in "flattened" organisations. It will be recalled that the mono-cultural and monochromatic conduct of IBM staff led nearly to the company's demise in the late 1980s and early 1990s.

The factors that delineate the research dimension–managing inter-subsidiary mandates–comprise variables of autonomy and/or dependence in headquarter-subsidiary relations in terms of: the extent to which the degree of maturity in the firm's internationalisation is influential in autonomising the subsidiary; the extent to which the complexity of subsidiary operations, R&D, manufacturing, etc., is a moderating variable in the dependency of subsidiary on parent MTNEs; the extent to which variety in subsidiary's relations in international sourcing as opposed to local sourcing is an intervening variable in the dependencia of subsidiary on HQ. It is worth noting that while some preliminary work has been performed on German and Japanese MTNEs (Taggart and Hood, 1999), there is a lack of corroborating evidence for Atlantic MTNEs or international firms from Pacific Newly Industrialising Economies (NIEs).

The factors that delineate the research dimension–managing intra-organisational inter-faces–consist of variables of de-verticalisation of knowledge creation. The world's MTNEs are dominated by Atlantic MTNEs (firms from North America and Western Europe) and distinctiveness is no longer at the centre of organisations but is increasingly at the periphery and sub-contracted. The issues therefore revolve around the ability of, and criteria used by, executive management to decide what constitutes a core operation and what should be created either inside or outside the firm. A poignant example is illustrated by the processing of airline ticket documentation for Swiss Air that is carried on in Bombay irrespective of where the ticket is purchased and used. Another is the sub-contract manufacturing of electronic components in South East Asia by world-class factories that are necessarily exposed to the R&D of principals and have patent sharing agreements with their clients.

The factors that delineate the research dimension–managing global treasury operations–are embodied by variables that describe ultimately the "boundaries" of the firm. In the context of the thousands of JIBAs among the relatively few MTNEs, firstly, these variables are operationalised by how "boundaries" are decided, formed and shaped in terms of communications, design and integration. Secondly, in terms of co-ordination mechanisms to signal the value of the firm's intermediate products and services and the control agency and instrumentation employed for compliance.

CONCLUDING REMARKS

To re-emphasize, the increase in global JIBAs means that an examination of the relationship organograms of the world's leading firms in airline, auto-aerospace, electrical-electronic, mineral and pharmaceutical sectors, shows that, practically speaking, they are all one company per sector. And these do not include the peculiar forms of the Japanese *Keiretsu* or South Korean *Chaebols* that are lattice relationships par excellence.

While a viable research agenda should aim at ascertaining determinants and dimensions to the issues indicated, the important point of relevance should be adhered to closely in any research. Firstly, relevance is in terms of the fact that SMEs are often the creators of employment and, in total, have a greater "surface area" to engage in economic transactions. Being "plugged" into the IISPMNs of MTNEs is crucial. The nature of intermediation has changed and, if the characteristics of how MTNEs manage, co-ordinate and integrate their dispersed intra-firm sub-contracting can be better appreciated by academicians and practitioners alike then this will be of material value to the growing numbers of internationalising SMEs to more usefully engage with MTNEs. Secondly, in the longer term, the research agenda may yield modest contributions to the theory of international business, entreprenuership and the dynamics of organisational evolution in an era of alliance capitalism and networks. Such additions to theory and literature orbit the dilemma–flexible co-ordination or efficiency within geo-economically dispersed MTNEs.

A tentative model of these relations to be examined has at its centre "strategic coherence" and on its periphery the four identified domains: managing intra-corporate culture; managing inter-subsidiary mandates; managing intra-organisational inter-faces; and managing global treasury operations. A model of these relationships is shown below in Figure 1.

FIGURE 1. A Model for Researching International Business Strategic Coherence

THE EMERGENT RESEARCH AGENDA

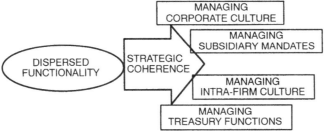

REFERENCES

Antonelli C., 1999, The evolution of the industrial organisation of the production of knowledge, *Cambridge Journal of Economics*, Vol. 23, No. 2, pp. 243-260.

Bartels F. L., Mirza H., 1999, Multinational corporations in Asia's emerging markets: Before and after the economic crisis–Any changes?, *Management International Review* (forthcoming Vol.).

Blanc H., Sirra C., 1999, The internationalisation of R&D by multinationals: A trade-off between external and internal proximity, *Cambridge Journal of Economics*, Vol. 23, No. 2, pp. 187-206.

Boddewyn J. J., Brewer T. L., 1994, International business-Political behaviour: New theoretical directions, *Academy of Management Review*, Vol. 19, No. 1, pp. 119-143.

Borys B., Jemison D. B., 1989, Hybrid arrangements as strategic alliances: Theoretical issues and organizational combinations, *Academy of Management Review*, Vol. 14, April, pp. 234-249.

Cohendet P., Kern F., Mehmanpazir B., Munier F., 1999, Knowledge coordination, competence creation and integrated networks in globalised firms, *Cambridge Journal of Economics*, Vol. 23, No. 2, pp. 225-241.

Colvin G., 1999, The year of the megamerger, *Fortune*, Vol. 139, No. 1, 11th January, pp. 32-55.

Conner K. R., 1991, A historical comparison of resource-based theory and five schools of thought within industrial organization economics: Do we have a new theory of the firm?, *Journal of Management*, Vol. 17, No. 1, pp. 121-154.

Dunning J. H., 1988, The eclectic paradigm of international production: A restatement and some possible extensions, *Journal of International Business Studies*, Vol. 19, No. 1, Spring, pp.1-31

Dunning J. H., 1994/95, Globalization, Economic Restructuring and Development, Univ. of Reading, Dept. Econ., Discussion Papers in International Investment and Business Studies, Series B, Vol. VII, p. 12.

Egelhoff W. G., 1991, Information-processing theory and the multinational enterprise, *Journal of International Business Studies*, Vol. 22, No. 3, 3rd Qtr, pp. 341-368.

Guéhenno J-M., 1995, The End of the Nation-State, University of Minnesota Press, Minneapolis.

Larson A., 1992, Network dyads in entrepreneurial settings: A study of the governance of exchange relationships, *Administrative Science Quarterly*, Vol. 37, pp. 76-104.

Porter M. E., 1990, The Competitive Advantage of Nations, Macmillan, London.

Spekman R. E., Isabella L. A., MacAvoy T. C., Forbes T., 1996, Creating strategic alliances which endure, *Long Range Planning*, Vol. 29, No. 3, June, pp. 346-357.

Spekman R. E., Forbes T. M., Isabella L. A., MacAvoy T. C., 1998, Alliance management: A view from the past and a look to the future, *Journal of Management Studies*, Vol. 35, No. 6, November, pp. 747-772.

Sriram V., Krapfel R., Spekman R. E., 1992, Antecedents to buyer-seller collaboration, *Journal of Business Research*, Vol. 25, No. 4, pp. 303-321.

Taggart J., Hood N., 1999, Determinants of autonomy in multinational corporation subsidiaries, *European Management Journal*, Vol. 17, No. 2, pp. 226-236.

Teece D. J., 1992, Competition, cooperation, and innovation: Organizational arrangements for regimes of rapid technological progress, *Journal of Economic Behavior and Organization*, Vol. 18, pp. 1-25.

Thurow L. C., 1999, Building wealth: The new rules for individuals, companies and nations, *The Atlantic Monthly*, June, Internet Version, http://www.theatlantic.com/issues/99jun/9906thurow.htm, accessed 20th September 1999.

UNCTAD, 1997, World Investment Report 1997, Transnational Corporations, Market Structure and Competition Policy, UN, UNCTAD, NY.

UNCTAD-ICC, 1998, The Financial Crisis in Asia and Foreign Direct Investment, Internet Version, http://www.unctad.org/en/pressref/bg9802en.htm.

UNCTAD, 1999, Global Foreign Direct Investment Boomed in 1998 Fueled by Mergers and Acquisitions in Developed Countries, Press Release, TAD/INF/2810, 22nd June, Internet Version, http://www.unctad.org/en/press/pr2810en.htm, accessed 20th September 1999.

World Bank, 1999, Global Development Finance 1999, World Bank Group, Washington, DC.

Determinants of Time-Span to Foreign Market Entry

Rod B. McNaughton

SUMMARY. The short time-span between start-up and foreign market entry observed for some small firms poses a challenge to the widely accepted characterization of small firm internationalization as an incremental process. This paper contributes to the study of early internationalization by empirically testing hypotheses about firm, market, product, and management characteristics thought to be associated with the time-span to foreign market entry. The hypotheses are tested using information from a mail survey of Canadian micro-firms that export manufactured goods. The results show that the small firms most likely to enter a foreign market early are new ventures with a knowledge intensive product selling in a niche market with few domestic competitors but numerous foreign ones. The interpretation is that these firms are influenced to internationalize by the need to reach markets of sufficient size, and to appropriate the benefits of their knowledge through first-mover advantage. These results support several basic propositions developed from the literature on early internationalization. They also help to identify situations in which entrepreneurs should consider early internationalization as a strategy. *[Article copies available for a fee from The Haworth Document Delivery Service: 1-800-342-9678. E-mail address: <getinfo@haworthpressinc.com> Website: <http://www.HaworthPress.com>]*

KEYWORDS. Internationalization, strategy, micro-firms, foreign market entry

---

Rod B. McNaughton is affiliated with the University of Otago, New Zealand.

[Haworth co-indexing entry note]: "Determinants of Time-Span to Foreign Market Entry." McNaughton, Rod B. Co-published simultaneously in *Journal of Euromarketing* (International Business Press, an imprint of The Haworth Press, Inc.) Vol. 9, No. 2, 2000, pp. 99-112; and: *Global Marketing Co-Operation and Networks* (ed: Leo Paul Dana) International Business Press, an imprint of The Haworth Press, Inc., 2000, pp. 99-112. Single or multiple copies of this article are available for a fee from The Haworth Document Delivery Service [1-800-342-9678, 9:00 a.m. - 5:00 p.m. (EST). E-mail address: getinfo@haworthpressinc.com].

INTRODUCTION

An emerging issue in the literature on small firm internationalization is the short time-span before some new firms enter foreign markets. Traditional models characterize the process of small firm internationalization as either a learning sequence (e.g., Johanson and Wiedersheim-Paul, 1975; Johanson and Vahlne, 1977), or a series of stages (e.g., Bilkey and Tesar, 1977; Reid, 1981) implying that international activities develop incrementally over time. These models implicitly assume that firms establish themselves in the domestic market before entering foreign ones (Oesterle, 1997, 126). However, the empirical evidence is that both the speed and complexity of firm internationalization is increasing, and a small but important proportion of firms is international from inception (e.g., OECD, 1997). The extant literature also contains an implicit assumption that firms must achieve a certain size in the domestic market before exporting. However, the empirical research relating firm size to export intensity has not produced consistent results. There are some small firms, and even micro-firms, that are heavily dependent on foreign sales (Vozikis and Mescon, 1985). Thus, while models that characterize internationalization as an incremental process may explain the "traditional" path of internationalization, some small firms pursue a different (accelerated) path (Madsen and Servais, 1997, 579). These firms present a challenge for existing theories of internationalization (Oviatt and McDougall, 1997).

Current understanding of the phenomenon of early internationalization is strongly influenced by the work of Oviatt and McDougall (1994) who attempt to integrate the international business, entrepreneurship and strategic management literatures to explain the phenomenon of international new ventures. Their work is primarily concerned with describing and explaining the existence of "born global" firms as an organizational form. Other approaches focus less on born global firms, and more on the speed or pace with which firms enter foreign markets. Examples include:

1. Oesterle's (1997) proposition that the quality of a firm's innovation is a strong influence on when internationalization begins;
2. Kutschker, Baurle and Schmid's (1997, 110-113) portrayal of the temporal dimension as a key to successful internationalization which needs to be actively managed in terms of order, timing, and speed; and,

3. Pedersen and Petersen's (1998) characterization of the issue as a matter of the pace of resource commitment to foreign markets.

The temporal dimension of the internationalization process is also evident in studies of first mover advantage, and in the notion that "momentum" is important to export development (e.g., Yang, Leone and Alden, 1992, 87).

Conceptual development (e.g., Oviatt and McDougall, 1994; Madsen and Servais, 1997), and case studies still largely dominate the literature on time-span to foreign market entry (see Table 1 in McDougall, Shane and Oviatt, 1994). This paper contributes to the development of this literature by empirically testing some basic hypotheses regarding the association between time-span to foreign market-entry and characteristics of the firm, its market, product, and management approach. The hypotheses are tested using information from a mail survey of the owners/managers of Canadian micro-firms that export manufactured products. Results are summarized in Table 1 below. Micro-firms represent a ". . . diverse small business microcosm at the beginning end of the stages of development theory, which does not conform to the crude generalizations of the broad theory" (Vozikis and Mescon, 1985, 60). Thus, they form a sampling frame in which examples of both incremental and early internationalization are found.

TABLE 1. Employment, Sales and Age Characteristics of Responding Firms

Characteristics of firms	Mean	Median	Standard Deviation	Maximum
Employment				
working owners	1.6	2	0.9	6
full time employees	1.0	0	2.2	14
part time employees	1.5	1	1.8	10
Sales ($CAN)				
most recent fiscal year	$97.5K	$100K	$58.8K	$300K
previous fiscal year	$69.3K	$60K	$62.3K	$450K
change (%)	225%	25%	1189%	9900%
export intensity (%)	45.3%	40.0%	32.7%	100.0%
years since establishment	8.6	6	10.4	64

The results provide useful empirical evidence for continued development of theories of early internationalization. They also help entrepreneurs to identify situations in which early internationalization is a strategy that should be considered.

HYPOTHESIS DEVELOPMENT

The emerging literature on early internationalization was recently reviewed by Madsen and Servais (1997) and thus need not be described in detail here. The essence of the argument arising from this literature is that a set of "pre-conditions" has developed that create an environment in which early entry into foreign markets is a strategy that may be successfully pursued by some small firms. The preconditions include changes in market conditions (especially specialization, flexibility, and global sourcing), changes in production, communication and transportation technologies, and the accumulation of human capital that is positioned to take advantage of these changes in markets and technology (Madsen and Servais, 1997, 565-567).

While there is general agreement that these forces are speeding the internationalization paths of some small firms, the situations in which the forces are most influential are not well understood. This research starts with the proposition that most small manufacturing firms are formed for the purpose of commercializing an innovation (a new product or improved process). The preconditions cited above make it possible for many products to be commercialized within a small firm. Oesterle (1997) argues that the quality of the innovation and the structure of its market strongly influence when internationalization begins. Thus, the time-span to foreign market entry is a key variable of commercialization strategy, and relates to the marketing issues of market selection and timing.

This perspective suggests a number of hypotheses about the situations in which a short-time span to foreign market entry is likely. First, as early entry is fostered by certain pre-conditions, the influences of which are fairly recent, new ventures are more likely to pursue this strategy than are firms established some years ago (H_1) (Oviatt and McDougall, 1997, 90). Second, market conditions such as specialization, flexibility and global sourcing result in attempts to commercialize increasingly niched or customized products (Madsen and Servais, 1997, 576-577). The markets for such products may be of insufficient size to meet growth (or even survival) objectives within Canada's relatively small economy. These markets might best be described as globally dispersed nodes. Thus, it is expected that early entries are more likely when the domestic market is small (H_2). A market characterized by globally dispersed nodes of demand is also likely to be characterized by transnational networks at both firm and individual levels. To successfully commercialize a product, a firm must participate in this international network (Johanson and Mattsson, 1988). This leads to the hypotheses that early entry is likely associated with low levels of domestic competition (i.e., there are few domestic players in the market), but high levels of foreign competition (H_3 and H_4 respectively) (Madsen and Servais, 1997, 576; Pedersen and Petersen, 1998, 488).

A third consideration is the quality of the innovation, in particular the extent to which it is proprietary and whether or not it is the tangible outcome of significant new knowledge (that is otherwise an intangible source of value for the firm). These two properties are inextricably related as patents and copyrights signal the uniqueness of a product, and protect new knowledge from opportunistic use by other parties. However, patents and copyrights are often ineffectual, especially for small firms in foreign markets. An alternative protection is offered by first-mover advantage, whereby firms establish their own international presence quickly to exploit their knowledge before others appropriate it (Rao and Klein, 1994). Thus, early entry is expected to be associated with proprietary products (H_5), and with knowledge intensive products (H_6).

Finally, the extant literature on early internationalization places considerable emphasis on the characteristics of the founding entrepreneur, especially international experience, and personal networks (Oviatt and McDougall, 1997, 93-94). Individual characteristics are also credited with a role in the literature that attempts to distinguish exporting from non-exporting firms. As all of the firms included in this study export, the key is the extent to which the founding entrepreneur sees increasing foreign sales as an important part of their overall business strategy, thus providing momentum for export development (Yang, Leone and Alden, 1992, 87). Early entry is expected to be associated with an active internationalization strategy (H_7).

SURVEY OF MICRO-EXPORTERS

A sample of micro-exporters was identified using the Business Opportunity Sourcing System (BOSS), an online database of Canadian exporters maintained by the Department of Industry, Science and Technology. (The name of this database was changed to Canadian Company Capabilities, and is now accessed via Industry Canada's Web site at *http://strategic.ic.gc.ca*). There are over 32,000 firms in this database, of which more than 21,000 are manufacturing firms. The primary purpose of the database is to help foreign customers identify Canadian firms that can provide particular products and services. The firms in the database are identified from industry directories, federal contract listings, trade associations, and business development programs. Listings are updated by an annual questionnaire. Calof (1994) used the BOSS database in a study of firm size and export propensity among manufacturing firms. He found that BOSS lists 53% of all Canadian manufacturing firms, but that the database is biased toward inclusion of larger firms. This is an artifact of the data collection procedure, which favors larger firms that have survived for some time.

There are 442 manufacturing firms that fall in the smallest size category of the BOSS (less than $CAN100K in annual revenues). This is a small proportion of the firms of this size in Canada, and likely represents much less than half of those in this size class that export. The owners or managers of the listed firms were contacted by mail for pre-notification, questionnaire delivery, and follow-up. From the original 442 mailings, 22 (5%) were returned as undeliverable, 28 (6%) were returned incomplete (most frequently because the firm did not export), and 75 were returned with complete information (17%). While the rate of return for useable responses is low, the number returned incomplete suggests there was significant target error in the original sample (i.e., inclusion of firms that do not export). The median firm had current sales of $CAN100,000, rapid sales growth (25%), two working owners, one part-time employee, and six years of operating experience (Table 1). These firms are also highly dependent on export markets, with a median of 40% of current sales from outside Canada. As the result of growth, the responding firms were larger than expected from the BOSS listing. The median value rather than the maximum value of the distribution of sales is $CAN100K.

Information was collected for individual export transactions, defined as the export of a product to a particular geographic market. Data for each transaction included the year of market entry, contribution to total sales, distribution channel used, and whether unsolicited orders preceded market entry. A total of 236 transactions were recorded, a mean of 3.1 per firm. The U.S. was the first market entered for 89% of the responding firms, and accounts for 54% of all of the markets served (Table 2). To better reflect the size and diversity of the U.S. market, respondents were asked to indicate if their firm entered all regions of the U.S. simultaneously (i.e., the national U.S. market) or if their firm concentrated on one or more regions. To define regional markets within the U.S., the questionnaire included a map of the nine major U.S. census regions, and the largest urban markets in each region. The first market entry occurred on average after 2.9 years of operation, and there is no statistically significant difference in the mean entry time between markets. When all market entries are consid-

TABLE 2. Timing of Market Entries

Region or country	First foreign market entry		All foreign market entries	
	Number of entries	Mean time to entry (years)	Number of entries	Mean time to entry (years)
1. All U.S.	25	3.2	25	3.2
2. Atlantic	23	2.2	36	3.4
3. Central	10	4.0	37	5.1
4. Pacific	7	2.5	30	5.0
5. EU	3	3.5	36	7.5
6. Asia	3	3.0	15	10.5
7. Other	4	1.7	57	8.2
Total	75	2.9	236	6.1
ANOVA	$F = .41$		$F = 3.51$	
	$p = 0.87$		$p = 0.00$	

1. Entry into all U.S. census regions almost simultaneously. The U.S. is treated as one market, rather than as a collection of regional markets.
2. Entry into New England, Middle Atlantic and/or South Atlantic census regions.
3. Entry into East North Central, West North Central, West South Central and/or East South Central census regions.
4. Entry into the Pacific and/or Mountain census regions.
5. Entry into one or more countries in the European Union.
6. Entry into one or more Asian countries, especially Hong Kong or Japan.
7. Entry into one or more other countries, particularly Australia and Scandinavian countries.

ered, however, there is a statistically significant difference in entry times, with entry into Asia, the European Union, and "other" countries being later. The pattern for most firms was to enter the U.S. first, and then overseas markets at a later time. The majority of first market entries were through direct exporting (64.6%), with the remainder being through agents/distributors (27.7%), licensing (1.5%), and dual channels (6.2%). If all market entries are considered, these percentages change slightly to direct (60.2%), agents/distributors (28.5%), licensing (4.5%), and dual channels (6.8%).

MEASUREMENT OF VARIABLES

The dependent variable, time-span to foreign market entry, was calculated by subtracting the year in which the firm was founded, from the year in which the firm entered its first export market(s). In a large number of cases exports were initiated in either the first (25.0%) or second year (21.9%) of operation. Unfortunately, because of the way time-span to foreign market entry was calculated, firms that were international from inception could not be distinguished from those that internationalized during their first year of operation. There is a break in the distribution, with a smaller number of firms starting to export in each of the third through eighth years (42.2%), and then a scattering of time-spans greater than eight years (10.9%). The relative lack of long time-spans is partly due to the distribution of the age of firms, which has a median of six years. As noted earlier, sampling very small firms increases the likelihood of observing start-ups. Firms that initiated export activities in their first or second year are termed "early exporters," their third through eighth years "average," and eight or more years "late exporters."

Respondents were asked to indicate the size of the domestic market (many customers, some customers, very few customers) and the level of competition they experience in both Canada and in their foreign markets (high, medium or low). They were also asked to state the number of direct customers and competitors that they are aware of in each market. In both domestic and foreign markets there is a statistically significant difference between the mean numbers of both customers and competitors when categorized by levels of the categorical measure, suggesting that the categories are valid.

Information was requested about the products that the firms produce. The firms generally had a single product, although in a few cases the "product" is actually a cluster of very similar items (e.g., several kinds of herbal tea). A wide variety of products are represented including industrial machinery and parts, consumer goods, food products, electronics and instruments, medical devices, and software. Respondents were asked to characterize the product as to whether it is "traditional" (68.2%) or "knowledge intensive" (31.8%), and whether or not it was proprietary in the sense of being protected by patent or copyright (67.7% are proprietary). Respondents were also asked if their approach to export development was best characterized as "active" in the sense that increasing foreign sales is an important part of their overall business strategy, or "passive" in that increasing foreign sales is not of primary importance (66.7% had an active approach). Finally, if the firm is a new venture or not was determined by its age, with firms less than eight years old at the time of the survey being classified as new ventures (63.0% were new ventures).

RESULTS

To evaluate the effect of the explanatory variables on time-span to first foreign market entry, an Analysis of Tables (ANOTA) model was applied to the responses. ANOTA is a computationally simple method developed by Keller, Verbeek and Bethlehem (1984) for the analysis of contingency tables with one nominal variable (Y) to be explained by a set of nominal variables ($X_1, \ldots, X_m$). The ANOTA model provides the linear main effects model for the expected proportions of Y, given $X_1, \ldots X_m$, based on ordinary least squares estimates. ANOTA translates a series of bivariate contingency tables ($Y \times X_m$) into tables of regression coefficients, where the effect of category j of X_m on category i of Y is standardized for the effects of all other explanatory variables in the model. Thus, ANOTA provides a convenient method for summarizing the relationships in a large number of bivariate tables, while controlling for potential interactions between the independent variables (see Clark, Deurloo and Dieleman [1988] for a comparison of ANOTA with alternative methods of analyzing categorical data). Moreover, this estimation method does not require full tables, allowing estimates to be generated for a relatively large number of parameters from a modest sized sample. This is the key reason for the use of ANOTA in this research as there are only 75 available cases. Unfortunately, no overall measure of fit has been developed for ANOTA models. However, standard errors can be calculated for individual parameters, allowing the hypothesis to be tested that a parameter estimate is significantly different from zero.

The parameters of the ANOTA model are shown in Table 3. The constants simply reflect the relative distribution of cases between levels of the dependent variable. ANOTA coefficients may be added together for combinations of independent variable categories to predict their aggregate influence on the dependent variable. Thus, for example, early entry into a foreign market is significantly associated positively with new ventures, very few customers, high levels of competition in the foreign market, and knowledge intensive products. It is negatively associated with established firms, high levels of competition in the domestic market, and low levels of competition in foreign markets. Further, the coefficient associated with any particular catego-

TABLE 3. ANOTA Model of Time-Span to First Foreign Market Entry

Independent variables	Early entry	Average entry	Late entry
Constant	46.9	42.2	10.9
Age of firm			
New venture	**5.8**	2.8	**−8.6**
Established firm	**−9.4**	−4.6	**14.0**
Size of domestic market			
Many customers	−2.2	−4.1	**6.3**
Some customers	−1.7	−1.3	3.0
Few customers	**12.0**	1.5	**−13.5**
Level of domestic competition			
High	**−18.4**	**29.6**	**−11.2**
Medium	8.1	**−12.7**	4.7
Low	8.9	**−14.5**	5.6
Level of foreign competition			
High	**22.0**	**−18.6**	−3.4
Medium	−2.1	6.2	−4.1
Low	**−14.4**	5.6	**8.8**
Product is proprietary			
No	−8.7	10.0	−1.3
Yes	4.3	−5.0	0.6
Knowledge based assets			
Traditional	5.8	7.3	**−13.1**
Knowledge intensive	**14.2**	−11.2	−3.0
Management approach			
Passive	−0.8	2.9	−2.1
Active	3.7	−5.0	1.3

Parameters in **bold** are significantly different from 0.0 at $p = 0.05$.

ry can be interpreted as a deviation from the average, as the coefficients sum to zero across the categories of the dependent variable.

H_1 is supported, as early entry is positively associated with new ventures and negatively with established firms, while the reverse is true for late entries. H_2 is partially supported as early entries have a significant positive parameter for small domestic markets (but not a significantly negative one for large markets), while late entries have a negative parameter for small markets and a positive one for large markets. The results for H_3 are mixed. Early entry is negatively associated with high levels of competition in the domestic market, but it is not positively associated with low levels of competition. Average time-spans to entry are positively associated with high domestic competition and negatively associated with medium and low levels. Late entry is negatively associated with high domestic competition, but is not positively associated with low levels of competition. H_4 is supported, as early entry is strongly positively associated with a high level of competition in the foreign market and negatively associated with a low level of competition. Average time-spans are negatively associated with high levels of competition, and late entry is positively associated with low competition. There is no statistically significant support for H_5 (product is proprietary). H_6 is partially supported, as early entry is associated with knowledge intensive industries. Interestingly, traditional sectors are negatively associated with late entries. Finally, there is no support for H_7 (management approach). While the valence of the coefficients is in the direction specified by the hypotheses, their size is insufficient given the standard error to be significantly different from zero.

DISCUSSION AND CONCLUSIONS

The results are consistent with a number of hypotheses that have emerged in the literature on early internationalization. The overall image is that firms that internationalize early are most likely to be new ventures with a knowledge intensive product selling to niche markets characterized by high levels of competition in foreign markets. The argument is that early internationalization is a strategy that is adopted to overcome the limits of a small domestic market, capitalize on opportunities in an internationalized market, and appropriate the benefits of a knowledge-based product. An important outcome of this research for entrepreneurial practice is the description of market and industry conditions where early internationalization should be considered.

The finding that the managerial approach to export development is not significantly related to time-span to foreign market entry is inconsistent with the stress placed on this factor by the extant literature. One explanation may be that the crude measure used in this research does not capture essential differences in management approach. A second possibility is the importance of management approach in determining when foreign activities begin which may be confounded in the extant literature with the importance of management approach in determining if foreign activities will be initiated.

The responses to a number of open-ended questions about why firms started to export adds insight to these empirical findings. The most frequent comments reflect the unique niche of the product, and the need to export to gain access to market(s) of sufficient size. Example products include electronic components and scientific instruments, medical implants, and vertical market software products. A few respondents wrote that they entered the U.S. before developing the domestic market because they thought U.S. customers would be more receptive to their innovation. In this vein, the owner of one firm commented "Canadian consumers are slow to accept new ideas before purchasing–they instead wait and see if the product is acceptable in other countries before buying." Another firm was established in Canada even though there was no domestic market, because the raw inputs to its product have a low value to weight ratio and are expensive to transport.

A number of respondents also commented that while they had entered foreign markets quickly, their efforts to maintain momentum and expand into additional markets (usually outside the U.S.) were hampered by limited production facilities, and more generally constraints of time and financial resources. Lack of knowledge about overseas markets was not as limiting as sometimes thought. Several respondents wrote comments similar to ". . . ours is a close-knit industry–we know who our potential customers are world-wide. The problem is getting the time and money to get around to see them." This has implications for export development policies which are often designed around an implicit "stages model" and focus on providing information about overseas markets. Slightly over half (58%) of the firms had used a government export development program, and more than half of these had internationalized early. However, the programs used were almost exclusively ones that provide funding to attend trade fairs, accompany an international trade mission, or visit overseas markets.

The primary limitation of this research is that because of the sampling frame the population to which the results can be generalized is unknown (as is the size of that population). Successful small exporters are likely over-represented, as are new ventures. As Madsen and Servais (1997, 579-580) point out, very small firms are likely to have more diverse internationalization processes than larger small firms. Thus, the results may only be representative of micro-exporters. The Canadian context may also be unique because of the relatively small domestic market, and easy access under the North America Free Trade Agreement to the overwhelming large U.S. market. Thus, future research should build on this attempt to empirically test factors hypothesized to be associated with the time-span to foreign market entry by using larger and cross-national samples.

REFERENCES

Bilkey, W.J. and G. Tesar (1977), "The Export Behaviour of Smaller-sized Wisconsin Manufacturing Firms," *Journal of International Business Studies*, Spring/Summer, 93-98.

Calof, J.L. (1994), "The Relationship Between Firm Size and Export Behavior Revisited," *Journal of International Business Studies*, 25(2), 367-387.

Clark, W.A., M.C. Deurloo and F.M. Dieleman (1988), "Modelling Strategies for Categorical Data: Examples from Housing and Tenure Choice," *Geographical Analysis*, 20, 198-219.

Johanson, J. and L.-G. Mattsson (1988) "Internationalization in Industrial Systems–A Network Approach," in N. Hood (ed) *Strategies for Global Competition*, London, Croom Helm.

Johanson, J. and J. Vahlne (1977), "The Internationalization Process of the Firm: A Model of Knowledge Development and Increasing Foreign Commitments," *Journal of International Business Studies*, Spring/Summer, 23-32.

Johanson, J. and F. Wiedersheim-Paul (1975), "The Internationalization of the Firm: Four Swedish Case Studies," *Journal of Management Studies*, October, 305-322.

Keller, W.J., A. Verbeek, and J. Bethlehem (1984), ANOTA: Analysis of Tables, Voorburg, Netherlands Central Bureau of Statistics.

Kutschker, Michael, Iris Baurle and Stefan Schmid (1997), "International Evolution, International Episodes, and International Epochs–Implications for Managing Internationalization," *Management International Review*, 37(2), 101-124.

Madsen, Tage Koed, and Per Servais (1997), "The Internationalization of Born

Globals: An Evolutionary Process?," *International Business Review*, 6(6), 561-583.

McDougall, Patricia Phillips, Scott Shane and Benjamin M. Oviatt (1994), "Explaining the Formation of International New Ventures: The Limits of Theories from International Business Research," *Journal of Business Venturing*, 9(6), 469-487.

Oesterle, Michael-Jorg (1997), "Time-span Until Internationalization: Foreign Market Entry as a Built-in Mechanism of Innovations," *Management International Review*, 37(2), 125-149.

Organization for Economic Co-operation and Development (1997), Globalization and Small and Medium Enterprises, Paris.

Oviatt, Benjamin M. and Patricia Phillips McDougall (1994), "Toward a Theory of International New Ventures," *Journal of International Business Studies*, 25(1), 45-64.

Oviatt, Benjamin M. and Patricia Phillips McDougall (1997), "Challenges for Internationalization Process Theory: The Case of International New Ventures," *Management International Review*, 37, 85-99.

Pedersen, Torben and Bent Petersen (1998), "Explaining Gradually Increasing Resource Commitment to a Foreign Market," *International Business Review*, 7, 483-501.

Rao, P.M., and Joseph A. Klein (1994), "Growing Importance of Marketing Strategies for the Software Industry," *Industrial Marketing Management*, 23 29-37.

Reid, S.D. (1981), "The Decision-maker and Export Entry and Expansion," *Journal of International Business Studies*, 12, 101-112.

Vozikis, G.S., and T.S. Mescon (1985), "Small Exporters and Stages of Development: An Empirical Study," *American Journal of Small Business*, 10, 49-64.

Yang, Yoo S., Robert P. Leone, and Dana L. Alden (1992), "A Market Expansion Ability Approach to Identify Potential Exporters," *Journal of Marketing*, 56, 84-96.

Overseas Trade Missions
as an Export Development Tool

Martine M. Spence

SUMMARY. Overseas trade missions provide SMEs with a privileged setting for gaining insights into foreign markets. The primary objective of overseas trade missions is to increase the flow of bilateral trade (Hibbert 1990) and as such, these events are often subsidised by governments. The administration of overseas trade missions varies with countries and depends on the countries' trade priorities and traditions. This paper proposes a trade mission process diagram explaining the various activities and decisions exporting SMEs are involved in prior, during and after trade mission participation. Interviews with executives suggest that specific performance objectives are set prior to the missions and relevant information is gathered during the whole process. First-hand market information provides small exporters with an in-depth understanding of foreign markets and helps them allocate their scarce resources to areas that present most potential. *[Article copies available for a fee from The Haworth Document Delivery Service: 1-800-342-9678. E-mail address: <getinfo@haworthpressinc.com> Website: <http://www.HaworthPress.com>]*

KEYWORDS. Exporting, internationalisation, overseas trade missions, export development

INTRODUCTION

In spite of advances in technology which allow firms to gain instant access to customers around the world, international travelling remains

---

Martine M. Spence is affiliated with Middlesex University, England.

[Haworth co-indexing entry note]: "Overseas Trade Missions as an Export Development Tool." Spence, Martine M. Co-published simultaneously in *Journal of Euromarketing* (International Business Press, an imprint of The Haworth Press, Inc.) Vol. 9, No. 2, 2000, pp. 113-125; and: *Global Marketing Co-Operation and Networks* (ed: Leo Paul Dana) International Business Press, an imprint of The Haworth Press, Inc., 2000, pp. 113-125. Single or multiple copies of this article are available for a fee from The Haworth Document Delivery Service [1-800-342-9678, 9:00 a.m. - 5:00 p.m. (EST). E-mail address: getinfo@haworthpressinc.com].

a necessity to thoroughly understand foreign customers' varied and specific needs. Visiting overseas markets provides executives with insights into business customs, legal and structural requirements, as well as shape their abilities to deal with differences. The acquisition of experiential knowledge, that is, a thorough understanding of the inner working of a foreign market, can only happen through direct experience with this market and maintaining a long term relationship with its actors. The importance of gaining such experiential knowledge has been acknowledge by a number of authors (Denis and Depelteau 1985, Reid 1984) and by governments alike. Most governments subsidise exploratory trips to foreign markets with the objective of encouraging SMEs to export to these markets. Overseas trade missions are part of the range of government-sponsored international trade promotion programmes available to SMEs. In spite of their wide use and the positive feedback received from participating firms (NAO 1996), these events have attracted little research from academics and practitioners.

This paper, therefore, proposes to give an overview of overseas trade missions and to assess their use as an export development tool for SMEs. First, the role of trade missions is explained and the various forms trade missions can take in various countries is looked at. The paper then focuses on the organisation of trade missions in the UK. Finally, a trade mission process diagram is suggested, based on qualitative interviews with recent trade mission participants.

TRADE MISSIONS COME IN DIFFERENT GUISES

Most governments, both in developed and developing countries, subsidise trade missions as part of the range of international trade promotion programmes offered to their domestic SMEs (Seringhaus and Rosson, 1991). According to Hibbert (1990), the primary objective of trade missions is to improve the flow of bi-lateral trade between two trading nations. To this end, trade missions provide a controlled and personalised setting that facilitates the assessment of market opportunities, the establishment of direct contacts with people of influence, and the access to prospective partners and customers (Seringhaus 1987).

The most extensive empirical studies about the role of overseas trade missions have been carried out by Seringhaus (1984), Seringhaus and Mayer (1988), and Seringhaus and Rosson (1990). Trade missions provide participants with experiential knowledge and as such have often been described as market entry facilitators (Seringhaus 1989). By allowing the gathering of first-hand knowledge about the target market, trade missions successfully fulfil market entry information needs for SMEs. Research by Seringhaus (1987) showed that the following types of information gathering can be carried out through trade missions:

- Hands-on information on market opportunities, product ideas, competitors;
- Up-to-date data about the market environment through direct personal contacts with potential customers, agents, industry associations, government officials;
- Exchange of experience with other participants;
- Evaluation of distribution and sales opportunities in target market;
- Increased visibility in target market through high level contacts attracted by mission organisers.

Furthermore, trade mission participants pointed out that trade missions are used as an "ice-breaker" into markets about which little is known. Trade missions also provide increased personal safety to participants due to numbers and sponsorship from a foreign government in markets where security may be at stake.[1]

Several types of government-subsidised trade missions can be identified. Outward missions generally consist of groups of domestic business persons travelling to foreign markets to collect market intelligence or sign contracts. In contrast, inward missions are designed to attract groups of foreign buyers or influencers. Their purpose is to meet with potential suppliers or influence the purchase of domestic goods.

Outward missions are called horizontal missions when the group consists of companies from various industry sectors. When participating firms are from the same industry sector, these missions are called vertical missions. Vertical missions are organised when the market presents specific opportunities in targeted industry sectors. These are generally set up by trade associations. Ministerial missions are outward missions led by a minister and to which high profile companies

---

1. This information was gathered during the author's participation in trade mission pre-departure briefing meetings in London.

are invited to participate. They might lead to large bi-lateral co-operation projects being signed.

TRADE MISSIONS AROUND THE WORLD

Similar programmes are offered in many countries to provide domestic firms with the opportunity to acquire experiential knowledge about foreign countries. The most popular of these programmes are trade fairs and trade missions. Although the objectives for trade missions pursued by most governments are similar, the way trade missions are administered and organised vary between countries. A variety of approaches to trade missions are offered by governments:

- In the UK, trade missions are part of a public-private partnership. Trade missions are subsidised by the Department of Trade and Industry (DTI) and sponsored by Chambers of Commerce and Trade Associations. The sponsors' role is to publicise and administer the events, recruit participants, arrange travel packages, and organise pre-departure briefing-meetings and field programmes. The majority of such trade missions cover a wide range of industry sectors; only a few are sectoral.
- Conversely, other countries like Belgium seem to favour ministerial trade missions and trade missions presided by HRH Prince Philippe, who is the Honorary President of the Office Belge du Commerce Extérieur (OBCE) (OBCE 1996).
- Spain emphasises inward trade missions to a greater extent than other countries. Among the 299 missions organised in 1995, 154 were inward trade missions and 145 were outward. Outward trade missions can have different focus–110 of them were direct missions, the objective of which is the same as the British ones, 26 were study trade missions aimed at trade associations, and 9 were mission-exhibitions with the purpose of exhibiting products in relevant venues (hotels, commercial centres). Direct trade missions can accommodate from as few as 2 participants to over 30 (ICEX 1996).
- In the US, trade missions are sectoral. They usually consist of groups of 5 to 12 business executives travelling to targeted overseas markets. The US government also offers Matchmaker Trade Delegations which are designed to introduce new-to-export or

new-to-market firms to prospective representatives overseas (Department of Commerce 1996).

• In France and Canada, a travel grant is given to firms to visit foreign markets on an individual basis. In Canada, collective trade missions are for new-to-export firms to the US, Mexico and Western Europe. In France, collective trade missions are not offered or funded by the government but might be by Chambers of Commerce or Trade Associations.

The Canadian government recognises the need for long term planning. Subsidies for the acquisition of experiential knowledge are only granted following approval of a detailed one-year marketing plan for a specific market. The government subsidises 50 percent of the costs of eligible activities to implement this plan. Some of the eligible activities include participation at trade fairs, international travelling, and adaptation of the marketing mix (DFAIT 1995).

ORGANISATION OF TRADE MISSIONS IN THE UK

In the UK, the objectives of outward trade missions are "to encourage small and medium-sized enterprises with fewer than 500 employees and firms new to exporting to explore overseas markets through missions sponsored by Trade Associations, Chambers of Commerce or similar organisations" (DTI 1996, p. 85). The scheme applies world-wide with the exception of Western Europe. A travel grant is paid to one representative from each company taking part in the mission. Some restrictions apply as to the frequency of participation: each firm is granted support for up to ten missions, of which no more than three can be to the same country (five in Japan). In some instances, such limitations have been met with resentment on the part of the users (Runiewicz 1994, 1995).

Budget for the Outward Missions Scheme and the number of participating companies increased more than any other programmes between 1990/91 and 1994/96 (Table 1). However, cuts were experienced for the years 1996/97 and 1997/98. Although the number of missions remained the same, the number of participants each sponsor could recruit for a mission was reduced from 30 to 15 in some markets. Impacts of these cuts on sponsors could result in increases in management fees and adverse publicity as some firms could be turned down as potential participants.

TABLE 1. Selected DTI Overseas Services–Expenditure and Outputs 1990/91-1995/96

Programmes	1990/91	1991/92	1992/93	1993/94	1994/95	1995/96	% Increase 1990/91- 1995/96
Overseas Trade Fairs							
Expenditure (£ million)	15.9	13.8*	13.2	13.5	17.1	19.8	24.5
Number of exhibitions	291	335*	325	282	334*	NA#	14.8
Participants	6611	7000*	7013	6439	8021*	NA	21.3
Outward Missions							
Expenditure (£ million)	1.1	0.8*	1.3	1.6	1.5	2.0	81.8
Number of missions	133	120*	122	127	149*	250*	88.0
Participants	1725	2000*	2271	2478	2450*	3500*	102.9
Inward Missions							
Expenditure (£ million)	0.8	0.8*	0.6	0.6	0.5	0.9	12.5
Number of missions	53	65*	46	33	34*	NA	(35.9)
Participants	578	650*	584	341	397*	NA	(31.3)
Overseas Seminars							
Expenditure (£ million)	0.3	0.3*	0.4	0.3	0.3	0.4	33.3
Number of seminars	19	23*	20	20	16*	NA	(15.8)
Participants	284	310*	299	246	320*	NA	12.7
Store Promotion							
Expenditure (£ million)	1.1	1.1*	0.7	0.6	0.5	0.6	(45.5)
Total supported	25	25*	18	11	13*	NA	(48.0)
Export Marketing Research							
Expenditure (£ million)					1.1	0.8	
Total offers of support					197	160	

Sources: DTI Annual Reports 1992 to 1996.
* Estimate
# Not Available

Interviews with trade mission managers provided an understanding of the organisation of trade missions in the UK. Every year, sponsors are recruited by the DTI through a formal twelve-month bidding process. Sponsors are selected for their expertise and experience in the target markets (Balabanis and Crilly 1996). When organising trade missions, sponsors try to include a variety of activities to enhance the objective and experiential knowledge acquisition of participating companies and their visibility in the market.

Four to six weeks before the event, objective knowledge about the targeted markets is provided to participants through a pre-departure briefing meeting. DTI country desk representatives as well as executives with experience in the markets give information about the countries' economic, political and cultural environments as well as business opportunities. Trade mission participants are given a briefing pack containing country profiles and other relevant information for their journey. Before leaving on the trade missions, staff at the British Embassy is at their disposal to provide them with additional information as required. To promote trade missions in the target market, a brochure including participants' details and firms' activities is produced and sent to relevant business contacts in the target market.

Another briefing meeting organised by the overseas post staff will take place soon after arrival in the country. It is followed by a reception, the purpose of which is to meet foreign and British government officials and local business persons in a social setting. Participants are asked to provide the British Embassy with a list of contacts to invite to the reception and it is one of their tasks upon arrival to follow-up on the invitations. It has generally been noted that, the higher the ranking of the officials attending the reception, the more relevant the contacts generated, as more decision-makers attend. Sometimes, a press conference can be organised by the overseas post staff.

Trade mission participants must spend a minimum number of days in the country in order to qualify for the grant. During that time, they are free to conduct business as they please. They also have to attend a de-briefing meeting before leaving the country. During this de-briefing meeting an informal evaluation of the trade missions is carried out. Participants are encouraged to use the flight and hotel(s) arranged by the sponsor to enhance positive group synergy and facilitate exchanges of market intelligence between group members.

TRADE MISSION PROCESS DIAGRAM

Further insights into SMEs' motivations to participate in trade missions were gained through qualitative interviews with executives that had recently participated in trade missions organised by the London Chamber of Commerce and Industry (LCCI). These executives travelled to various destinations in Latin America, Africa, Asia, the Middle-East, Eastern Europe and the Mediterranean region and were interviewed soon after their return. These interviews were conducted with 11 participants either by telephone or face-to-face depending on the geographical locations of the firms and lasted between half an hour to two hours.

Before the decision to participate in a trade mission is made, firms need to conduct a thorough audit of their human and financial resources and to assess their ability to meet potential demand in the foreign market (Barrelier et al. 1992, Hollensen 1998). This was supported by one of the participants who stated: "Before talking about trade mission, a firm has to be set-up for exporting. It has to have a product or service which is exportable."

Firms' specific characteristics in terms of size, core business activity, past experience and acquired knowledge may influence the trade mission process (Aaby and Slater 1989, Axinn 1988, Madsen 1989, Miesenbock 1989) (Figure 1, Box 1). Firms react to internal and external stimuli (Box 2) and develop perceptions on the potential of various markets (Box 3) (Katsikeas 1996, Malekzadeh and Rabino 1986). When firms are seriously interested in a market and feel there is potential, they may want to investigate this market further through a visit (Box 4). The visit could either be an individual one (Boxes 5, 6, 7) or the exporters could join a trade mission (Box 8). Trade mission participants mentioned that their main reasons for using the scheme was to explore a market in which they had not previously done business, to find new contacts, to conduct market studies, and to establish or revive agencies.

It has been demonstrated that exporters using trade missions as an export entry strategy are more systematic, research and planning oriented than non-users (Seringhaus and Mayer 1988). The participants confirmed these findings and stated that they would carry out as much research as possible before the trade missions (Box 9). The sources of information used depended on the level of involvement the firms have already had with the market. When firms have already been doing business with the market, they look at internal data to evaluate the extent of their efforts and the results generated. They also collected sector-specific data from the target market. When firms were new to the market, general data about the country's economic and political situation were gathered from various sources (such as market reports, articles, and people with experience in the market).

Firms also went to considerable efforts to find suitable lists of customers and agents and to set up appointments before the trade missions. At this stage firms may have used the DTI services, or they may have obtained information in more creative ways. For example, a firm manufacturing labelling machines for the pharmaceutical industry contacted the head-offices of their customers in London and asked about the activities of their subsidiaries in the targeted markets. This same firm also contacted suppliers of products complementary to their own

FIGURE 1. The Overseas Trade Mission Decision-Making Process

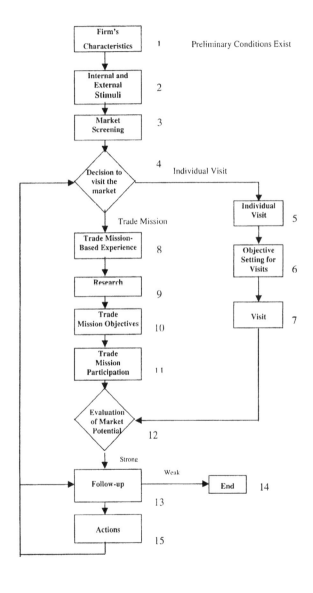

for the pharmaceutical industry and visited potential customers with the suppliers. When agencies were already established, firms arranged appointments with potential and existing clients through their agents.

Based on the information gathered before the trade missions, participants set objectives that may be used as benchmarks to evaluate trade mission outcomes once the events are over (Box 10). Participants mentioned that trade missions should be used when firms are in the early stages of working with a country. Trade missions are not suitable when business is well established in the market, or when the agencies are working properly. In these cases, the intricacies of working with a market are well known and the agencies provide the necessary support to conduct business profitably. One of the participants indicated that "the main reason for using a mission on a follow-up trip would be financial."

Trade missions have been shown to be market entry facilitators (Seringhaus and Mayer 1988). This was supported by the respondents who reported gaining a detailed knowledge of the market through the information provided by both the organisers and the market (Box 11). This information gathering was both formal and informal. Objective market specific information is first provided formally through a number of meetings. The trade missions also provided an informal and comforting environment for the participants as they travelled with other business persons from their own country who speak the same language. As a result, exchanges were facilitated, both at the social and business levels. It was mentioned that "the intensity of the programme obliged (participants) to go and talk to as many people as you can" while individual visits would only encourage going to existing contacts.

After the events, participants conducted an evaluation of the results they achieved during the trade missions (Box 12). A holistic approach was taken to evaluate trade mission performance, as a number of factors contributed to their overall satisfaction with the experience. The participants also differentiated between trade mission performance and export performance. Respondents have indicated that trade mission performance could be evaluated on the quality of contacts made, the quality of enquiries received, the type of market information gathered, the opportunity to strengthen existing relationships, and whether their objectives had been achieved. As one respondent stated:

> Evaluating trade mission performance is the most difficult thing in the world. Evaluating trade mission performance on the number of orders would be wrong. There is no absolute terms of

evaluation for 12-18 months after. I would look at the number of useful contacts in the right areas, the potential to do business.

Most respondents measured export performance in tangible terms: sales and profitability. The main difference was in the time participants expected performance to come about. Some of them had a long term approach and accepted that further investment in time may be needed before tangible business could be generated. Others expected profitability in the short term. The difference in outlook was mainly industry-dependent.

After the trade missions, participants conducted a routine follow-up with the contacts they met during the trade missions and their agents (Box 13). Within one to three weeks, a courtesy letter to all contacts, even if not potential, was sent. Also, additional information was provided: samples, quotes, brochures. A follow-up fax may have been sent three months later. Further visits to the market were primarily dependent upon the potential business that may be generated. Some participants left with a more positive view of the market, others felt that the market was not yet ready for their products. As a consequence, they did not take any further actions in the market and they directed their efforts to countries with more potential (Box 14).

The contacts met during the trade missions provided participants with "first-hand experience on the ground." They could assess people on the way they worked, and they had "real contacts, face-to-face." This helped participants to modify their approach in the market and more precisely tailor their products and services to customers' needs (Box 15). For example, one firm used the trade mission to reactivate business in the market. Their presence in the country as well as personal contacts with their agents helped them understand what was wrong in their relationship with their agency. Consequently, they could reach a consensus to take corrective actions.

CONCLUSION

The experiential knowledge firms acquired during the trade missions provided SMEs with a realistic overview of market requirements and potential, and a better understanding of the competition. As a result, and in some instances, the products were modified. For example, one respondent started manufacturing a lower range of valves, without compromising on safety, to be able to meet the competition from emerging economies. Their original valves, that meet ISO 9000 standards and are mainly sold in Europe, are too expensive for less industrialised countries. Some respondents also felt that amendments to their promotional material was required, especially translation into a foreign language. However, if market potential was perceived as poor at the time of the mission, SMEs' scarce resources were directed more profitably to other markets.

The knowledge acquired from the information gathered prior to the trade missions, from the market itself through direct contacts with local business persons, and from the reactions of these individuals within the following months, led trade mission participants to better decision-making and resource allocation. Any decision to repeat the process, from visiting the market to committing further resources to it, would be based on the participants perception of market potential. This evaluation of market potential would be based in large part on the experiential knowledge acquired during the missions, but would remain primarily subjective at this stage.

The suggested diagram (Figure 1) of trade mission process was part of a wider investigation into the evaluation of trade missions. Further research should aim at operationalising some of the variables suggested by the respondents, and more specifically the variables evaluating trade mission and export performance and assessing the objectives for the visits.

This diagram should also be tested empirically through a quantitative survey with recent trade mission participants. The result could be aimed at highlighting the significant variables that influence the trade mission process, and trade mission outcomes as well as export performance following trade mission participation.

REFERENCES

Aaby, N.-E. and Slater, S. (1989). Management influences on export performance: A review of the empirical literature 1978-1988. *International Marketing Review*, 6 (4), 7-26.

Axinn, C. (1988). Export performance: Do managerial perceptions make a difference? *International Marketing Review*, (Summer), 61-71.

Balabanis, G. and Crilly, M. (1996). Developing and managing trade missions in Britain: An organisers' perspective. Proceedings of the Academy of International Business Annual Conference, Birmingham: March 29-30.

Barrelier, A., Duboin, J., Duphil, F., Gevaudan, N. and Grataloup, L. (1992). Exporter: Pratique du Commerce International (9th Ed.). Paris: Editions Foucher.

Denis, J.-E. and Depelteau, D. (1985). Market knowledge, diversification and export expansion. *Journal of International Business Studies*, (Fall), 77-89.

Department of Commerce (1996). Export Programs: A Business Guide to Federal Export Assistance Programs (PEMD). Washington, D.C.: U.S. Government Printing Office.

Department of Foreign Affairs and International Trade (DFAIT) (1995). Program for Export Market Development. Ottawa: Government of Canada.

Department of Trade and Industry (DTI) (1992). British Overseas Trade Board Annual Report 1991/1992 and Forward Plan. London: HMSO.

Department of Trade and Industry (DTI) (1994). British Overseas Trade Board Annual Report 1993/1994 and Forward Plan. London: HMSO.

Department of Trade and Industry (DTI) (1996). British Overseas Trade Board Annual Report and Forward Plan 1995/1996. London: HMSO.

Hibbert, E. (1990). The Management of International Trade Promotion, London: Routledge.

Instuido Espanol de Commercio Exterior (ICEX) (1996). Memoria de Actividades 1995. Madrid: Ministerio de Comercio y Tourismo.

Katsikeas, C. (1996). Ongoing export motivation: Differences between regular and sporadic exporters. *International Marketing Review*, 13 (2), 4-19.

Madsen, T. (1989). Successful export marketing management: Some empirical evidence. *International Marketing Review*, 6 (4), 41-57.

Miesenbock, K. (1990). Small business and exporting: A literature review. *International Small Business Journal*, 6 (2), 42-61.

National Audit Office (NAO) (1996). Overseas Trade Services: Assistance to Exporters, London: HMSO, April.

Office Belge du Commerce Extérieur (OBCE) (1996). Le Commerce Extérieur et L'OBCE en 1995. [Supplément aux Informations du Commerce Extérieur]. Bruxelles: Office Belge du Commerce Extérieur.

Reid, S. (1984). Information acquisition and export entry decisions in small firms. *Journal of Business Research*, 12, 141-157.

Runiewicz, M. (1994). The Second Survey of International Services Provided to Exporters. London: The Institute of Export and NCM Credit Insurance Ltd.

Runiewicz, M. (1995). The Third Survey of International Services Provided to Exporters. London: The Institute of Export and NCM Credit Insurance Ltd.

Seringhaus, R. (1984). Government export marketing assistance to small and medium-sized Ontario manufacturing firms: The role and impact of trade missions on firms' off-shore market involvement. Ph.D. Dissertation, York University.

Seringhaus, R. (1987). The use of trade missions in foreign market entry of industrial firms. *Industrial Marketing and Purchasing*, 1 (3), 43-60.

Seringhaus, R. (1989). Trade missions in exporting: State of the art. *Management International Review*, 29 (2), 5-16.

Seringhaus, R. and Mayer, C. (1988). Different approaches to foreign market entry between users and non-users of trade missions. *European Journal of Marketing*, 22 (10), 7-18.

Seringhaus, R. and Rosson, P. (1990). The impact of government export promotion programmes: A case study. In R. Seringhaus and P. Rosson (Eds.), Government Export Promotion: A Global Perspective, London: Routledge, 222-246.

Seringhaus, R. and Rosson, P. (1991). Export Development and Promotion: The Role of Public Organizations, Norwell, MA: Kluwer Academic Publication.

Index

<c

operation and outcomes, 66-68
research method, 61-62
Joint International Business
Assocations (JIBAs), 88,89,
90-91,92,93
Joint ventures, 88

Knowledge, market, 45-46

Location Specific Advantages, 90

Marketing
networks and global orientation,
5-7
niche, 1-10
symbiotic between small and large
firms, 7-9
Market internationalisation, 25
Market knowledge construct, 45-46
Markets, psychically distant, 42-43,
53-56
Microexporters, New Zealand survey
of, 99-111. *See also*
Time-span determinants
Middlesex University (England),
113-125
Monopolistic advantage/market
imperfection theory, 2-3
Multi-Transnational Enterprises
(MTNEs), 85-97
conclusions, 94-95
global market of, 87-89
implications of research agenda,
91-94
literature of and lacunae in, 89-90
research agenda pertaining to,
90-91

Nanying Business School (Singapore),
85-97
Network relationships construct, 46-47

Networks
marketing studies of, 5-7
New Zealand study of impact,
37-57
organisational as compared with
personal, 27-28
role of for small business, 20
New ventures. *See* Start-ups
New Zealand study of networks, 37-57
central research hypothesis, 41-43
conceptualisation of concepts, 45-47
discussion, 54-56
findings, 48-54
literature review, 38-40
method, 43-45
Niche marketing, 1-10
Norwegian School of Management,
59-84

Oaten hay JAG (joint action group),
66-67,71-72,73-74,76-77.
See also Joint Action Groups
(JAGs)
Oligopolitic reaction theory, 3
One World Alliance (airlines), 9
Organisational characteristics, as
antecedents of
internationalisation, 25-28
Organisational networks, 27-28
Orientation
global, 5-7
international, 27
(University of) Otago (NZ), 99-112
Out-sourcing, 1-10
Overseas trade missions and, 113-125
decision making in, 121
forms of, 114-116
process diagram for, 119-123
in United Kingdom, 117-119
worldwide comparison of, 116-117

Performance, internationalisation,
23-24,28-29
Pre-export behavior model of
internationalisation, 39

*For Product Safety Concerns and Information please contact
our EU representative GPSR@taylorandfrancis.com Taylor & Francis
Verlag GmbH, Kaufingerstraße 24, 80331 München, Germany*

T - #0060 - 160425 - C0 - 212/152/8 [10] - CB - 9780789013026 - Gloss Lamination